DISABILITY, CUL
Alfredo J. Artiles and Elizabeth B. Kozleski, Series Editors

Does Compliance Matter in Special Education?

IDEA
and the
HIDDEN
INEQUITIES
OF PRACTICE

CATHERINE KRAMARCZUK VOULGARIDES

TEACHERS COLLEGE PRESS

TEACHERS COLLEGE | COLUMBIA UNIVERSITY
NEW YORK AND LONDON

Published by Teachers College Press, 1234 Amsterdam Avenue, New York, NY 10027

Library of Congress Cataloging-in-Publication Data

Names: Voulgarides, Catherine Kramarczuk, author.
Title: Does compliance matter in special education? : IDEA and the hidden inequities of practice / Catherine Kramarczuk Voulgarides.
Description: New York, NY : Teachers College Press, [2018] | Series: Disability, culture, and equity series | Includes bibliographical references and index. |
Identifiers: LCCN 2018001356 (print) | LCCN 2018009582 (ebook) | ISBN 9780807776889 (ebook) | ISBN 9780807759011 (pbk.) | ISBN 9780807759028 (case)
Subjects: LCSH: Children with disabilities—Education—United States. | Educational equalization—United States. | United States. Individuals with Disabilities Education Act.
Classification: LCC LC3981 (ebook) | LCC LC3981 .V68 2018 (print) | DDC 371.90973—dc23
LC record available at https://lccn.loc.gov/2018001356

ISBN 978-0-8077-5901-1 (paper)
ISBN 978-0-8077-5902-8 (hardcover)
ISBN 978-0-8077-7688-9 (ebook)

Printed on acid-free paper
Manufactured in the United States of America

25 24 23 22 21 20 19 18   8 7 6 5 4 3 2 1

I dedicate this book to you, Cielle.
Never forget to take your passion and
use it to make the world a better place.

Contents

Preface

Prior to engaging in the research that shaped this book, I was a middle school special education teacher. The first class I ever taught was a self-contained 12:1:1 classroom in Washington Heights in the northernmost part of Manhattan, New York City. This means that my classroom had one teacher (me), a paraprofessional, and a maximum of 12 students labeled with mild to moderate disabilities.

On my first day of teaching I walked into my 7th-grade 12:1:1 classroom and met the 6 boys, the youngest being 16 years old, and one girl I would be teaching for the school year. Nearly every student I had in the class was labeled either earning disabled, mentally retarded (now referred to as intellectually disabled) and/or emotionally disturbed. I was charged with teaching them 7th-grade social studies, science, and math (when the administration needed me to). I was not properly trained, but I was there and they were my students. To say the least, it was a challenge. But that class, and the students I taught in subsequent years, changed my life for the better, both professionally and personally.

As a teacher, I learned to give my students the space to tell me their stories so I could learn who they were. My students gave me their hopes, their dreams, and most important, language to understand how they experienced schooling. I learned about them and their families and I learned with them every single day. However, I also learned that every September I was guaranteed a class comprised mostly of young men of color who were classified with a disability, and that I wouldn't have enough resources to support my students in the way that I wanted to. I also found myself wondering if I was giving my students what they actually needed to succeed.

While teaching I felt like I was constantly juggling the need to understand my students' academic and social needs, while questioning whether or not my students actually had a disability or if they were in special education because of missed educational opportunities. I felt like my students' parents and I were trying to learn what the Individuals with Disabilities Education Act (IDEA)—one of the most influential pieces of federal education legislation in the United States—could do for their children, but resources were always scarce. I also found myself needing to comply with IDEA, but also constantly facing a seemingly insurmountable bureaucracy and excess of paperwork that diverted me from the substantive aspects of teaching and learning that would help my students succeed. By the end of my third year of teaching, I realized that I was asking myself over and over again the following question in the pursuit of educational justice: *Does compliance matter in special education?* And, in complying with IDEA, was I actually serving my students in the best way possible? Or was I complying to comply?

While I clearly know that compliance matters and that IDEA is an incredibly important piece of legislation, I also know that decades of research have shown that special education has not equitably served all the students it should. Wealthier—and often, white—students tend to receive the best services through IDEA, while racialized inequities continue to surface in special education outcomes. It is this reality and contradiction, coupled with the question that perplexed me when I was a teacher—*Does compliance matter in special education?*—that eventually led me to design and conduct this study.

Acknowledgments

I am incredibly privileged to have had professional mentors pushing me to look at and understand educational inequality and inequity from different perspectives. Each perspective has given me the critical insights that I needed to bring this book to fruition. I am grateful for all of them.

In particular, I'd like to thank Dr. Pedro Noguera. He is a powerful force in education; one of the greatest honors I've had as a doctoral student was to be a student of his. Under his mentorship I learned how to refine my academic voice, and he pushed me to never forget that my work has to be relevant to educators. I want to also thank Dr. Lisa Stulberg for her patience, compassion, and steady belief in my progress. Under her mentorship I came to a clear understanding of what it means to be a sociologist of education, where social theory and educational practice are equally important in academia. My thanks also to Dr. Richard Arum for pushing me to never forget the importance of social theory. Under his kind, yet clear, mentorship I learned to think analytically and systematically about complex social issues. I also want to thank Dr. Edward Fergus. Without his leadership as the deputy director at the Metropolitan Center for Urban Education while I was at New York University, I would never have gotten the chance to learn what it means to be an applied researcher working for educational equity in special education. In addition, dispersed throughout this book are pieces of a paper that Dr. Fergus and I wrote together with Dr. Kathleen King Thorius, which serves as a testimony to his influence on my work. I also want to thank Mark Alter for his unwavering support as I pursued my doctorate. He constantly challenged me to think about the purpose of special education and to never forget that purpose.

I want to thank Dr. Alfredo Artiles for listening to my ideas while simultaneously pushing me to stretch my thinking in ways that I never could have anticipated. His vision and critical insights related to special education, culture, and equity are invaluable. Alex Aylward, a colleague and good friend, has been an incredible collaborator. Throughout the years she has supported me and pushed my thinking, and has always been open to finding new ways to look at complex research problems. I want to thank Dr. Adai Tefera for the thoughtful conversations we had about special education, policy, research, and life in academia. And thank you to Sarah Diaz and Lisa Jackson for your support and dedication to equity research.

I am lucky to call many dedicated educators and equity consultants good friends. Our friendships are nourishing. I want to specifically thank Natalie Zwerger, Lorraine Lopez-Janove, and Traci Anderson for their unwavering support and belief in me and my work, and in the power and potential of students. You are inspirational people. And thank you to Teachers College Press for helping me bring this book to life, in particular Brian Ellerbeck, Jamie Rasmussen, and Lori Tate.

I want to acknowledge the students that have forever touched my heart. My work in education began with my first teaching job in Washington Heights, New York City. It was there that this journey, this book, and my personal and professional life turned toward directly serving students and becoming a lifelong educator. I owe much to the late Ourrania Pappas for letting me experiment with Ms. "Jam" and create a special education program that introduced me to some of the most amazing people I have had the privilege to teach. In particular, Daniella, Domingo, and Erica: I constantly kept the three of you in mind as I wrote this book, and in addition to your resilience, love, and honesty as human beings in a very complicated world.

I am grateful to my family. I couldn't be where I am without you and your unwavering commitment to education and the lifelong pursuit of becoming a better person. My mom and dad, my brothers and sisters, Irene, Alex, and Bina, you have always been there for me and you have always pushed me to be the best person I can be. Bianca and Stefan, your love and support are precious, thank you. You all believed in me when I needed it the most. Also, thank you, Brenda and Louis, for your support through the years. And to Baba, Bopsha, Jajo, Dido, and Walter, thank you for being my inspiration and for your steadfast dedication to the power of education. As Dido told my dad on their journey to the United States, "People may take things from you, but they can never take what is in your mind." Education can change the world.

It is with this last statement that I lead into the most important dedication of all. To Anthony, I thank you for being my rock and for traveling with me on this journey. Your dedication to your students and to the teaching profession inspires me every day. I watch you teach and work for your students and I know that everything you put into your work is changing the world for the better in some small way every day. I appreciate you and all you do. And to my Cielle, I work for you. I work to somehow make an imprint on this world so that you know how important it is to be a socially just, committed, and giving citizen. Our world needs you and you are my inspiration, hope, and fire.

Introduction

This is a book about racial disproportionality in special education and the Individuals with Disabilities Education Act (IDEA), the single most influential piece of legislation affecting students with disabilities in schools. It is also about the paradox that exists between the persistence of racial disparities in special education and an extensive legal framework aimed at ensuring equal opportunity and access to high-quality educational services for all students. In this book, I engage with the paradox and *theoretically* and *empirically* question how individual rights, protections, and monitoring of special education outcomes can coexist with persistent racial disparities. I also show how compliance with IDEA may not be enough to ensure that educational equity is achieved in practice.

WHAT IS DISPROPORTIONALITY?

Racial disparities in special education are formally known as disproportionality. The issue is defined by a group's over- or underrepresentation in an educational category, program, or service in comparison to the group's proportion in the overall population (Donovan & Cross, 2002). The educational trends that characterize disproportionate outcomes in special education parallel longstanding educational inequalities related to income, gender, racial, ethnic, and language differences, to name a few. Despite this fact, disproportionality is considered a special education issue because federal disability legislation has defined it, procedural remedies have been targeted to remedy it, and funds have been specifically allocated to address the issue through the Individuals with Disabilities Education Act (IDEA).

Public Law 94-142, also named the Education for All Handicapped Children Act (EAHCA, 1975), was passed by the U.S. Congress in 1975 and served as the legislative basis for IDEA. The EAHCA was later renamed IDEA in 1990. IDEA is a civil rights law based on the 14th Amendment, which ensures equal treatment of all U.S. citizens by providing equal educational opportunity to students with disabilities through a free appropriate public education (FAPE). The law was created to address and redress historical inequities associated with the education of students with disabilities

1

in schools across the United States, and it has governed how students with disabilities should be educated for nearly 4 decades (Minow, 2010).

TECHNICAL REMEDIES FOR ADDRESSING DISPROPORTIONALITY THROUGH IDEA

It was not until the 1997 reauthorization of IDEA that racial disproportionality was mentioned in the legislation, despite the fact that educational research had identified the issue as a civil rights concern since the 1960s (e.g., Dunn, 1968). The 1997 amendment of IDEA [20 U.S.C. §1418(c), 1998] established a specific policy approach for identifying disproportionality in special education and it included attention to data collection surrounding disproportionality:

> Each State that receives assistance under this part, and the Secretary of the Interior, shall provide for the collection and examination of data to determine if significant disproportionality based on race is occurring in the State with respect to (A) the identification of children as children with disabilities, including the identification of children as children with disabilities in accordance with a particular impairment described in section 602(3); and (B) the placement in particular educational settings of such children.

However, the regulations and guidance did not provide sufficient direction for what it meant to collect such information. In the March 1999 *Federal Register* (Vol. 64, No. 48) the Office of Special Education Programs (OSEP) clarified its approach for addressing disproportionality and asked states, in addition to collecting data on disproportionality patterns, to review their policies, practices, and procedures associated with IDEA implementation (Markowitz, 2002). Unfortunately, though, the 1997 regulations did not result in reductions in patterns of racial disproportionality (Albrecht, Skiba, Losen, Chung, & Middelberg, 2012; Hehir, 2002).

IDEA was again reauthorized in 2004 [20 U.S.C. §1412(a)(22, 24)], which further altered the educational policy approach for addressing disproportionality.[1] Per the 2004 reauthorization, states have to monitor special education outcomes through 20 quantifiable and qualitative indicators [20 U.S.C. 1416(a)(3)], known as State Performance Plan (SPP) indicators.[2] Three SPP indicators are specifically related to disproportionality:

- Indicator 9 refers to the disproportionate representation of racial and ethnic groups in *special education and related services* that is the result of *inappropriate identification*.
- Indicator 10 refers to disproportionate representation of racial and ethnic groups in *specific disability categories* that is the result of *inappropriate identification*.

- Indicator 4 has two components:
  - » 4A refers to significant discrepancies in the rates of long-term suspensions of students with disabilities compared to districts in a state.
  - » 4B refers to significant discrepancies in the rates of long-term suspensions of students with disabilities, based on race and ethnicity, compared to districts in a state *due to inappropriate policies, procedures, or practices.*

Two different, and potentially unintended, definitions of disproportionality were included in the 2004 legislation (Skiba, 2013). The first is "*significant disproportionality*," which is determined by a numerical threshold that is set by each state education agency (SEA) that alerts to disproportionate outcomes; it includes only issues of overrepresentation of racial and ethnic groups in special education outcomes, and it does not consider whether or not compliance with IDEA is achieved. The second definition, "*disproportionate representation*," has been interpreted by SEAs and LEAs (local education agencies) as including issues of both over- and underrepresentation and it is related to a qualitative review of LEAs' policies, procedures, and practices related to IDEA administration and compliance with it (Skiba, 2013). The twofold approach results in districts first being numerically identified for disproportionality and then being subjected to compliance reviews by SEA representatives.

The twofold approach has proven highly problematic and ineffective (Albrecht et al., 2012) in addressing disproportionate outcomes. For example, Cavendish, Artiles, and Harry (2014) examined data from national annual performance reports (APRs) and found that many states established low thresholds for triggering disproportionality. State-level latitude has also resulted in significant variations across states as to what constitutes disproportionality (e.g., Albrecht et al., 2012; U.S. Government Accountability Office [GAO], 2013). For instance, the U.S. GAO (2013) reports Maryland, Iowa, and Louisiana identify districts as disproportionate based on a relative risk ratio numerical threshold of 2.0 or more, while South Carolina, California, Mississippi, and Connecticut use a 4.0 or more threshold. The U.S. GAO (2013) findings raise questions about whether or not IDEA policy provisions are adding to the disparate outcome because of the absence of clarity in the policy, processes, and formula.

On December 13, 2016, the U.S Department of Education once again announced regulatory changes to IDEA and disproportionality monitoring. The proposed changes "establish a standard approach that States must use in determining whether significant disproportionality based on race or ethnicity is occurring in the state and in its districts" as a direct response to the Government Accountability Office (GAO) 2013 report on differential disproportionality monitoring across the United States.[3] The changes are important; however, they were not relevant when this study took place. And in December of 2017, the Trump administration proposed either changing, delaying, and/or eliminating the proposed regulations, despite pushback from civil rights groups and educators.[4] This book will show, whether the current policy changes are implemented or not, that the technical and individualized nature of IDEA and its ideological foundation hinders educators' capacity to use IDEA to systematically address racial disparities in special education. This is despite the best intentions in people, policies, procedures, and educational practices.

THE LIMITS OF IDEA TO ADDRESS COMPLEX INEQUITIES

It is difficult for educators to use IDEA to address disproportionality because of the legislation's technical, individualized, race-neutral, and deficit-based foundation. Kramarczuk Voulgarides, Fergus, and Thorius (2017), in their review of remedies associated with addressing disproportionality through IDEA, find that although inclusion of disproportionality monitoring in IDEA recognizes the effect of race on special education outcomes, the remedies, procedural protections, and interventions embedded in IDEA do not explicitly attend to the impacts of racial, ethnic, and cultural differences and how they affect the schooling process; rendering a colorblind or race-neutral policy approach to address the complex educational issue. Colorblindness is characterized by a "denial and downplaying of racial inequality and racist practices" in everyday life (Doane, 2017, p. 946), despite the fact that racialized inequities are ever present. This policy approach deletes the sociological complexity of how "race" operates in society and it also negates the impact of social context and human interactions on the production of educational inequities.

In addition, since its inception IDEA legislation has relied upon a deficit model of disability, where disabilities reside within individuals and can be fixed through individualized educational remedies. This approach implies that "fixing" a child's academic and/or behavioral issues through individualized educational interventions is sufficient for addressing disproportionality.

A deficit framework is deeply embedded in false notions of meritocracy, because it places the responsibility of learning on individual bodies and does not sufficiently question how social structures, norms, and systems contribute to persistent inequalities in education. And it also—intentionally or not—locates the sources of academic failure and/or behavioral issues within students, their upbringing, or the families and communities that they come from (see Valencia, 2012; Valencia & Solórzano, 1997). Deficit frameworks and notions of meritocracy and individuality are embedded within the ideological framework of IDEA, as is a colorblind lens.

Smith and Mayorga-Gallo (2017) connect colorblind racial ideology to deficit frameworks and state, "colorblind racial ideology creates a façade of racial inclusion by suggesting that in a post–civil rights era, everyone has an equal opportunity to succeed, and if differences in outcomes across racial groups continue to exist, these differences are best explained through culture, natural occurrences, or 'a little bit' of residual racism that may still exist due to prejudiced individuals" (p. 891). Smith and Mayorga-Gallo (2017) describe how the combination of these two frameworks, deficit perspectives and colorblindness, imply that students' academic and/or behavioral failure(s) in school are their own fault and are not related to broader social and contextual forces or structural inequities.

Therefore, the convergence of technical, individualized, colorblind, and deficit frameworks in IDEA creates the conditions where good intentions in people, policies, procedures, and educational practices cannot ensure that equity is achieved for all students. This book examines why this happens. It also examines how these social forces converge, affect educational practice, and ultimately reproduce racialized outcomes in special education.

EXAMINING COMPLIANCE AND EQUITY IN EVERYDAY ACTIONS

Data for this book were gathered from a comparative ethnographic project that I conducted in the 2011–2012 academic year in three suburban school districts located in a large northeastern state. Each district included in this book had an extensive history of disproportionality citations.

Fieldwork took place over the course of the 2011–2012 academic year and involved approximately 1,200 hours of combined observations and interviews.[5] While in the field, I shadowed the district-level special education administrator in each of the three school districts. I chose to study district-level special education administrators because they communicate with their state education departments about compliance-related activities, are responsible for initiating and enacting changes related to their district's citation, and they oversee the majority of special education activities in schools.

The three districts that were included in this study varied in their free and reduced-price lunch status, achievement levels, student racial and ethnic compositions, and in their disproportionality citation status in the year of research (2011–2012 academic year). While all three districts had past histories of disproportionality citations (numerical threshold/*significant disproportionality*), they were in different phases of addressing their citations (review of policies, procedures, and practices/*disproportionate representation*). Figure I.1 summarizes the social context and citation data associated with each of the three districts that participated in the study: Gerrytown, Huntertown, and Sunderville.[6]

Figure I.1. Social Context and Citation Data

GERRYTOWN

Citation History

Cited for significant disproportionality in the year of research under Indicator 4.

The district had gone under a compliance review associated with disproportionate representation prior to the 2011–2012 school year.

The district was cited five times for Indicator 4A and/or 4B between 2004 and 2011.

Community Context	District Context
19,000 Residents	3,000 Total enrollment
41% white residents	7% white students
40% Black residents	56% Black students
19% Latinx residents	37% Latinx students
$80,000 Median income	65% of students qualified for free and reduced-price lunch
	Low-achieving district according to state math and English language arts tests
	Graduation rate: 88%
	Dropout rate: 2%
	Per pupil expenditures: $25,000
	Classification rate: 17%
	State average: 13%

SUNDERVILLE

Citation History

Cited for significant disproportionality in the year of research under Indicator 4.

The district had gone under a compliance review associated with disproportionate representation prior to the 2011–2012 school year.

The district was cited nine times for Indicator 4A and/or 4B and once for Indicator 10 between 2004 and 2011.

Community Context	District Context
40,000 Residents	9,000 student enrollment
79% white residents	64% white students
7% Black residents	15% Black students
14% Latinx residents	19% Latinx students

Figure I.1. Social Context and Citation Data

$77,000 Median income	33% of students qualified for free and reduced-price lunch
	Average achieving district according to state math and English language arts tests
	Graduation rate: 78%
	Dropout rate: 4%
	Per pupil expenditures: $20,000
	Classification rate: 13%
	State average: 13%

HUNTERTOWN

Citation History

Not cited for significant disproportionality in the year of research.

The district had lingering effects of a compliance review associated with disproportionate representation.

The district was cited three times for Indicator 9 between 2004 and 2011.

Community Context	District Context
11,000 Residents	1,650 Total enrollment
92% white residents	85% white students
1.5% Black residents	2% Black students
6% Latinx residents	11% Latinx students
$110,000 Median income	15% of students qualified for free and reduced-price lunch
	High-achieving district according to state math and English language arts tests
	Graduation rate: 100%
	Dropout rate: 0%
	Per pupil expenditures: $23,000
	Classification rate: 11%
	State average: 13%

*Information has been slightly altered to maintain anonymity of the study district and participants. All information was taken from the state's education website and the 2010 U.S. Census American Fact Finder.

Roger. In Gerrytown, I shadowed Roger Nero, the district-level special education administrator whom I came to know on a first-name basis. Roger worked in Gerrytown for many years prior to my arrival and had extensive experience responding to the state's mandates surrounding a citation for disproportionality. The district had a significant history with disproportionality and consistently vacillated between being cited and not cited for disproportionate outcomes in the suspension and expulsion of students with disabilities and for students with disabilities by race/ethnicity since the 2004 reauthorization of IDEA. In the year of research, the district was in the process of conducting a self-review of its policies, practices, and procedures associated with the discipline of students with disabilities. If, after this review, the district remained above the state's threshold for disproportionate outcomes in suspensions, state auditors would intervene and directly monitor district actions.

Roger told me that his "compliance efforts" resulted in "a good relationship" with the state auditor who monitored the district's actions. Roger also said that the state auditor praised him for having "the right mentality" when addressing disproportionality. Roger consistently tried to meet compliance demands by adopting intervention programs, conducting professional development with staff about compliance, and closely monitoring district outcomes related to suspensions in the district.

Marc. In Sunderville, I shadowed Marc Sown, the district's assistant director of special education. Marc was one of a three-person team of directors who oversaw the administration of special education services in the district. Marc was specifically charged with monitoring discipline in the middle and high schools and was also in charge of addressing compliance issues associated with the district's citation for disproportionality in suspensions. Melinda, the other assistant director of special education, oversaw the elementary school and instructional initiatives in the district. Lilla, the director of special education, broadly oversaw their work and directly collaborated with the superintendent, Dr. Lovene.

Sunderville School District had been cited for racial and ethnic disproportionality in special education nearly every year that the SPP indicators(s) had been in place, from 2004 to 2011. The district consistently vacillated between being cited for disproportionate outcomes in the suspension and expulsion of students with disabilities and for students with disabilities by race/ethnicity. The only aberration to the pattern occurred one year when the district was concurrently cited under both Indicator 4 and Indicator 10. In the 2011–2012 school year, the district was cited for its high number of suspensions and expulsions of students with disabilities by race/ethnicity.

While in the field, I learned that Dr. Lovene had hired Lilla because of her successful history of turning around struggling special education departments in other districts. Both Marc and Lilla were relatively new to

Figure I.2. Indicator 4 Areas of Targeted Review

- Review of student records to see if positive behavioral supports have been used
- Review of Individual Education Programs to determine any use of behavioral supports and interventions prior to suspension
- Review to determine if Behavioral Intervention Plans were developed and utilized
- Review to determine if Manifestation Determination hearings occurred prior to suspension or expulsion
- Review to determine if a proper interim alternative educational setting was provided for any suspended student

the district, having worked there for only 3 years, inclusive of the year of research. Prior to Marc and Lilla's arrival, the special education department suffered from years of leadership attrition. An employee who had worked in the district for over 25 years told me that the district "is and was cited on everything," because Sunderville "had eight or nine directors of special education in the past 25 years, and eight of them were within 10 years." He said that because of "so much chaos and turnover," people were left to follow "their own moral compass" in regard to compliance with IDEA.

Due to Sunderville's extensive citation history and its persistent issues with IDEA compliance, the district had already self-reviewed its policies and practices associated with SPP Indicators 4 and 10 prior to my time in the district. State auditors had also spent several years observing district practices and actively monitored the district's progress toward compliance. Compliance monitoring was a normal facet of life in the district.

Both Gerrytown and Sunderville were subject to a review of their policies, practices, and procedures related to Indicator 4 in the year of research. Figure I.2 outlines the areas of targeted review.

Cynthia. While in Huntertown, I shadowed Cynthia Stromlo, the district's special education administrator. The district had been cited for racial and ethnic disproportionality in special education for 3 consecutive school years for Indicator 9. Specifically, Huntertown was cited for the disproportionate identification of Black students in special education. When Huntertown was initially cited, the special education department, along with central administration staff, conducted a self-review of the district's policies and practices related to the classification of students with disabilities. However, after this review, the district remained numerically disproportionate and was subsequently subjected to state oversight of district practices in the following school year. The initial state audit indicated that the district was noncompliant with 3 of the 18 procedural regulations associated with

Indicator 9. In the year of research Huntertown's classification, numbers by race were just below the state's threshold for identifying disproportionality. Huntertown had successfully exited a citation (significant disproportionality); however, remnants of state oversight persisted in the areas of noncompliance that had been previously identified in the state review.

Cynthia had been working in the district for several years and had direct experience with addressing the district's citation. She was very passionate about her job and frustrated by the citation and the state officials who monitored her district. She thought the citation implied "negative and untrue things" about Huntertown. Cynthia would often tell me that Huntertown was a small district and that it was "frustrating" to get cited because "one Black family could move in or out of the district" and that could determine whether or not the district was cited for Indicator 9. The district's original citation was associated with the placement of approximate 20 Black students in special education. Figure I.3 outlines the areas of targeted review associated with Indicator 9.

Roger, Marc, and Cynthia all worked very hard for the students in their districts. Their stories, found in the pages of this book, are presented with the utmost respect for the hard work and dedication they exhibited toward the students and families they serve. Their stories are also honestly presented so that we, as educators, researchers, and policymakers, can relate to their experiences and better understand how, whether intentionally or not, our everyday acts of compliance with social and professional norms may actually produce and reproduce racial inequities.

ORGANIZATION OF THE BOOK

There are three big ideas that surface and resurface throughout the chapters of the book that illuminate the ways in which complex social forces, and our complicity with them, contribute to the persistence of racial inequities in special education. First, throughout I acknowledge that disproportionality is a complex problem that is related to social, historical, political, and economic factors. It cannot be solved solely through decontextualized and individualized educational interventions and/or policy prescriptions. Second, I constantly question what good intentions, in policies, people, and educational practices, can achieve when educators do not directly acknowledge the presence of racialized inequities. Lastly, in every chapter I decenter the idea that a legislative commitment to equal opportunity and access is sufficient for achieving equity in educational outcomes.

In Chapter 1, I provide a brief historical background of the civil rights history of IDEA. The chapter describes how the procedural emphasis of IDEA influences educational practice. It also outlines the equity implications

Figure I.3. Indicator 9 Areas of Targeted Review

- Review of schoolwide approaches and prereferral interventions
- Review of the referral process for students to special education
- Review of educational practices surrounding students with disabilities
- Review of the district's eligibility determinants for special education

---

of procedural compliance when IDEA is applied to practice.

Chapter 2 unpacks the sources of disproportionate outcomes and relates disproportionality in special education to broader educational opportunity gaps. Specifically, the chapter focuses on understanding how special education classification and placement processes, disciplinary practices, sociodemographic contexts, and segregated school systems relate to disproportionate outcomes.

In Chapter 3, I highlight how educational leadership, whether at the school or district level, greatly affects how educational inequities are either sustained or addressed within local contexts. In the chapter, I show how important it is for educational leaders to have a strategic equity vision to address disproportionality, because if they do not, educational inequities will flourish.

Chapter 4 explores the role that parents play when interfacing with IDEA. The chapter shows how parents have been given a pivotal role in the administration of IDEA mandates. However, there are broader social forces that differentially affect a parent's capacity to effectively advocate for his or her child via IDEA and through educational institutions. The equity implications of parental involvement are also discussed.

Chapter 5 examines the logic of compliance surrounding IDEA implementation. The chapter highlights how the procedural remedies in IDEA that are leveraged when a district is cited for disproportionality are limited in their capacity to address the complex issue. The chapter also examines how procedural compliance with IDEA can coexist with high numerical values of disproportionality.

The Conclusion defines the compliance paradigm that surrounds the delivery of special education services in schools across the United States. The chapter illustrates how the compliance paradigm constrains educators' efforts to effectively address a systemic inequity like racial disproportionality. The chapter also provides future policy-to-practice suggestions that challenge the compliance paradigm.

In summary, throughout the chapters of this book, I present some disturbing educational practices that I believe must be documented so that educators, policymakers, and researchers can better understand how personal discretion and policy mandates intersect and relate to persistent racialized inequities in special education. In addition, the themes that are raised in the six chapters of the book pose a dilemma that we all have to contend with, which is that unless we are intentional in our actions and actively challenge systems of inequity, we become complicit in the production of racial inequities. We must not do this, and we must all hold one another accountable for truly addressing racial inequities that manifest within our educational system.

HOLDING OURSELVES ACCOUNTABLE FOR INEQUITY

I close the Introduction to this book with a reflection on sociologist Charles Payne's work on educational inequality. I share Payne's (1984) work in order to make it clear how the stories within this book do not just represent a moment in time that we are reading about; they provide a mirror to broader issues that we, as educators, need to face in order to achieve equity in educational outcomes. I also share this work so that we don't assume that the stories of Roger, Marc, and Cynthia are unique to them and their contexts, but that they serve as insights into better understanding how our everyday decisions, orientations, and interactions relate to persistent racial inequities.

Charles Payne (1984), in his book on urban education, used the term *fragmentation of harm* to identify a social process where people working within organizations and schools produce intended and unintended disparate outcomes through chains of interactions that extend across different individuals, organizational units, and institutional boundaries. Fragmentation of harm is based on the Weberian idea that people in modern society are specialists who are embedded within bureaucratic systems and vast divisions of labor that make it relatively difficult for them to understand the aggregate impacts of their everyday actions on inequality. Under this framework, inequality is rationalized, as it seems to "just happen" (p. 38), leaving no one truly accountable for its occurrence. Payne (1984) offers the following analogy to illustrate his point about fragmentation of harm:

> During the Vietnam War era, a Jules Feiffer cartoon appeared that went something like this: A man working in a munitions factory explains that he is not killing; he's just trying to get out a product. The same goes for the man who crates bombs in that factory. He's just packaging a product. He's not trying to kill anyone. So it goes until we come to the pilot who flies the plane that drops the bomb. Killing anyone? Certainly not, he's just pushing a button. In the last panel there is a Vietnamese peasant, dead, but not killed, you might say. The consequence is there, but born of a process so fragmented as not to register in the consciousness of those involved in it. (p. 37)

Payne (1984) likens the message in the cartoon to the way in which individuals relate to their work in schools and to educational inequality. He argues that it is easier for an individual to focus on his or her own work rather than holistically understand how their actions relate to broader processes of harm and educational inequality. Payne states that although people may be conducting their work "with the best interests of those at hand" (p. 41) and to the best of their ability, the decisions and choices made in the course of a day may unintentionally harm, discriminate, deny, or give opportunity to one group or person over another and, over time, lead to unequal outcomes. Therefore, a key part of the notion of fragmented harm implies that inequality is sustained because either opportunities are not provided or systems of inequality go unchallenged or unquestioned (Pollock, 2010) in schools.

Therefore, while this book does not identify individual remedies or interventions that eliminate disproportionate outcomes, and it does not seek to find ways to "fix" students or "help" them learn, it does tell a story about the seemingly invisible ideological, social, and organizational forces that operate within educational systems and that contribute to our complacency in the production of disproportionate outcomes in special education. I hope that the message that comes from the pages of this book positively impacts the hearts and minds of its readers and ultimately leads to improvements in the conditions that promote educational equity and high-quality teaching and learning for *all* students.

CHAPTER 1

The Individuals with Disabilities Education Act

Enacting Equal Opportunity Through Procedural Compliance

Prior to the 1970s, there were virtually no federal or state laws protecting students with disabilities in the United States. Rather, people with disabilities were segregated, marginalized, excluded, and denied basic social and educational services (Winzer, 1993). Compulsory education laws, enacted in the 1900s, intensified the segregation and exclusion of students with disabilities in schools because the principles of compulsory attendance laws were at odds with the eugenics movement (Spaulding & Pratt, 2015). All the way up until 1969, "courts upheld legislation that excluded students whom school officials judged would not benefit from public education or who might be disruptive to other students" (Yell, Rogers, & Rogers, 1998, p. 220). It was not until after 1969 that the legislative climate changed for students with disabilities. This was related to growing social unrest about the unequal treatment of marginalized groups in the United States and to the legal and legislative victories of the civil rights movement. Specifically, the civil rights victories of the 1950s and 1960s for people of color and women helped ensure disability rights would become a priority for the U.S. Congress (Minow, 2010; Skrentny, 2009) and influenced the passage of Section 504 of the Rehabilitation Act of 1973 and the Education for All Handicapped Children Act (EAHCA), which eventually became IDEA.

CIVIL RIGHTS FOR STUDENTS WITH DISABILITIES

Section 504 was the first federal law in the United States that protected people with disabilities. This law took into account a nondiscrimination framework that was directly shaped by Title VI (Skrentny, 2009). Title VI is part of the Civil Rights Act of 1964 and prohibits discrimination based on race, color, and/or national origin in agencies that receive federal funds. In relation to schools, the passage of Section 504 ensured that a student with a disability would receive the educational accommodations and modifications necessary to have equal opportunity and access to the educational benefits afforded to a student without a disability.

The passage of Section 504 also mobilized disability rights advocates to work on further securing the educational rights of students with disabilities in schools. Disability rights advocates used the reasoning found in *Brown v. Board of Education of Topeka, Kansas* (347 U.S. 483) to shape their strategy, asserting that the segregation and exclusion of students with disabilities from educational services was a violation of equal protection and due process (Ong-Dean, 2009). This strategy helped shape the outcomes of influential court cases—*Pennsylvania Association for Retarded Children (PARC) v. Commonwealth of Pennsylvania* (334 F. Supp. 1257) and *Mills v. Board of Education of the District of Columbia* (348 F. Supp. 866)—which eventually led to the passage of IDEA.

The *PARC* case was centered upon gaining rights for mentally retarded children who were excluded from the educational system. The case established that schools should remedy the historical discrimination of mentally retarded children in schools by granting the plaintiffs equal protection and equal rights to public education under the 14th Amendment (Ong-Dean, 2009). *Mills* was a class-action suit brought on behalf of seven children who had been identified as having behavioral problems and as being mentally retarded. The suit claimed that the students were excluded and denied their rights to an education. *Mills* set the precedent that schools must provide public education to all children regardless of their disability. According to Ong-Dean (2009), the *PARC* and *Mills* courts "shared a fundamentally social orientation," establishing that students with disabilities were not solely defined by their disability, but were also subject to "the consequences of cultural prejudices and institutional deficiencies" (pp. 19, 20) within the education system.

PARC and *Mills* set the groundwork for passage of Public Law 94-142, also named the Education for All Handicapped Children Act (EAHCA) in 1975, later renamed IDEA in 1990. The EAHCA was the first broad legislative move by the U.S. Congress to hold state and local education agencies accountable for the education of students with disabilities under a nondiscrimination framework. *PARC* and *Mills* also provided the procedural and substantive framework for IDEA that still exists to date.

Unfortunately, though, the civil rights intent of IDEA (stemming from *Brown*) did not take a prominent role in the legislative development of IDEA. Zirkel (2005) states, "the IDEA itself, both currently and as originally passed in the form of the EAHCA, makes no mention of *Brown* in its findings or other provisions," further noting that Congress has focused on "procedural, rather than a substantive, standard of equal opportunity for students with disabilities, who had been denied access to education" (p. 263). The courts have also relied upon a logic of procedural compliance to ensure educational rights are met. For example, in *Board of Education of the Hendrick Hudson Central School District v. Amy Rowley* (1982), the *Rowley* court determined "the law's [IDEA] emphasis on procedural requirements reflected a 'legislative conviction' that the *substance* of an appropriate education would usually be realized by simply meeting the law's procedural requirements—in particular, the requirements for including parents in the formulation of the IEP [individualized education program]" (Ong-Dean, 2009, p. 32). The focus on procedural compliance and the use of individual rights–based language remains prevalent throughout both the 1997 and 2004 reauthorizations of IDEA.[1]

The procedural emphasis of IDEA has proven to be a legislative burden for SEAs and LEAs, as many are unable to achieve 100% compliance with IDEA (Stein, 2009; Wakelin, 2008; Wrightslaw, n.d.). Arguably, this may be true because educators are faced with the enormous task of ensuring that educational opportunity and access are achieved through IDEA, while working in an educational system that does not provide the conditions to achieve this ideal. The sources of this tension, and the reason why the ideals of IDEA cannot be realized in practice, are influenced by local contextual factors that complicate the policy implementation process.

POLICY IMPLEMENTATION WITHIN LOCAL CONTEXTS

Understanding the social mechanisms behind why seemingly good intentions in policy and practice do not manifest in equitable outcomes is extremely complicated. In the case of IDEA, one important factor to consider is that the policy implementation process is inherently messy. There are multiple human, organizational, and societal influences that distort a policy's intent when it is applied to practice, a process known as loose coupling (Weick, 1976). Loose coupling contributes to the production of inevitable yet unintended consequences that can either support or divert a policy's purpose (Sieber, 1981).

The policy implementation process is also complicated by the organizational contexts within which humans use a policy. For instance, individuals working within complex organizations such as schools must make decisions about educational practices, policies, and procedures with readily available yet imperfect information rather quickly—a form of bounded rationality (March & Simon, 1958). Bounded rationality is like a mental container that facilitates decisionmaking and human understanding of the world. However, it also leads to *satisficing* (March & Simon, 1958). When individuals *satisfice*, they pick and choose which information they have available to act upon in order to develop a solution so that they can maximize rewards and minimize the costs of their work. Essentially, when individuals satisfice, it makes their work more manageable even though satisfactory, not optimal, decisions are being made.

Bowker and Star (2000), in their work on classification systems, describe the process of satisficing as people not doing the "ideal job, but the doable job" (p. 24). They highlight how satisficing allows for unexamined biases to permeate decisionmaking processes because the "doable job" uses familiar and taken-for-granted social scripts to accomplish a goal. In a similar vein, Sterman's work (1994) on complex organizations, he highlights how individual worldviews permeate decisionmaking processes as "decisions are the result of applying a decision rule or policy to information about the world as we *perceive* [emphasis added] it" (p. 293). Satisficing does not require that assumptions, ways of being and operating, and/or actions be examined for their equity impacts. Thus, when someone satisfices, their workflow may become manageable, but a manageable and comfortable workload is not what is needed to increase educational opportunity and equity for all students.

Satisficing is also problematic because the policy implementation process does not occur in a decontextualized vacuum. It is influenced by local historical, political, economic, and social conditions that affect the schooling process. For instance, the policy implementation process is affected by the racial and economic context of a school and/or school district. In particular, school districts—whether they are urban, suburban, rural, or town-sized—are experiencing demographic shifts that have led to increased racial and economic segregation that affects student outcomes (Bohrnstedt, Kitmitto, Ogut, Sherman, & Chan, 2015; Frankenberg & Orfield, 2012; Fry, 2009). These shifting contexts influence how educators relate to students and how educational policies are used within local contexts. They also influence how educational resources are distributed to diverse students. For example, Evans (2007), in her study on a school experiencing demographic change, found that school personnel used seemingly nonracial discourse to draw distinctions between the *new* and *existing* students that connoted racial messages connecting whiteness with something "good" or "right" and relating "blackness" or "other-ness" to something "not so good" or "wrong" (p. 344). These connotations also influenced how educational resources were distributed to diverse students across the district.

Discriminatory social forces like the ones described in Evans's study operate on a daily basis in multiple contexts and affect how policies are leveraged, or not, to support students. They also influence how policies like IDEA are understood and used in everyday educational practice. For instance, in Sunderville, a racially and economically diversifying school district, the administrative team took on the burden of ensuring compliance was achieved at any cost because the district had a long history of noncompliance with IDEA. In Gerrytown, a racially and economically segregated school district, the weak connections between the school district and the local community affected how compliance was enacted in practice. Compliance with IDEA was often a symbolic and superficial act that did not serve students well. In Huntertown, a predominantly white and wealthy community, compliance was not at the forefront of educators' minds. Substantive compliance with IDEA was taken for granted as a given facet of district life. However, wealthier and often white students received higher-quality educational services in comparison to other students in the district. In summary, across all three districts, the balancing act between satisficing meeting the civil rights intent of IDEA and procedurally complying with IDEA had equity implications that could not be easily resolved because local contextual factors made it difficult for the educators in all three districts to adequately serve all students.

Sunderville: Procedural Compliance Is Nonnegotiable

The leadership team in Sunderville was very open about how much they struggled to "put the needs of the kids first," as Lilla often stated, and become compliant with IDEA. This was because achieving procedural compliance in Sunderville was like a cat and mouse game; the administrative team could never catch up to all of the noncompliance issues in the district. This was partly symptomatic of the years of leadership attrition in the special education department and partly symptomatic of the compliance demands associated with the administration of IDEA. Marc told me that he, Lilla, and Melinda were constantly trying to get IDEA "paperwork in line," and many of the administrative team's professional development sessions with staff focused on aligning staff resources to facilitate compliance with IDEA procedural mandates. When I asked Marc why the administrative team did this, he said, "We don't really have a choice" and "anything and everything we do is to prepare for litigation or state oversight" of the special education department's actions.

For instance, in the middle of the school year, I attended a 3-hour professional development meeting with all of the district's psychologists, which was led by Lilla, Marc, and Melinda. The administrative team spent almost the entire time instructing staff on how to correctly fill out an IEP and how to adhere to a new procedural mandate instituted by the state education department. Throughout the meeting the psychologists were visibly and vocally frustrated by the amount of time they had to use to complete paperwork associated with IDEA and by the lack of time they had to actually spend with students.

In particular, the psychologists were frustrated by Lilla and her administrative team's pressure to evaluate what seemed like "hundreds" of students, as one psychologist stated, in a very short period of time. The psychologists were being pressured to evaluate students because (1) many students in the district were not given IDEA-compliant evaluations in a timely manner, and (2) since the evaluations hadn't been conducted, the psychologists had to get all students' evaluations done within a 2-month period in order to appear compliant when state auditors visited the district. The resulting consequence was a profound tension between the civil rights intent to administer nonbiased evaluations and the need to *show* compliance to state auditors. These two forces were at odds with each other and seemed to thwart the best intentions of all the educators in the room. One psychologist even mentioned that he felt like he didn't want to see students because of the amount of paperwork that he would have to complete after meeting with a student.

Unfortunately, though, the administrative team consistently sidelined the psychologists' concerns related to substantive compliance with IDEA. Lilla, Marc, and Melinda were hyperfocused on achieving procedural compliance even though it seemed to thwart the civil rights intent of IDEA. For instance, during the PD nearly 90 minutes of heated discussion ensued between the psychologists and the administrative team about locating where a date and signature should be on an IEP. The meeting's participants seemed to be spinning in circles trying to understand why this administrative step had to be taken. Lilla had to forcibly interrupt the chatter after about an hour was spent on the matter. She stated, "Basically, we are doing this [going over procedures] to see how long we can run from the state" and "to avoid further audits," referencing the district's tendency to be audited by state officials for being noncompliant with IDEA. She reiterated, "We are solely doing this [going over procedures] for compliance purposes." She tried to empathize with the psychologists about the cumbersome nature and impact of the procedural mandates on their workflow, but she also made it clear that they had no choice but to focus on compliance.

The psychologists seemed to understand Lilla's explanation and had patience with her, but her explanation added to their growing exasperation. One psychologist asked her, "So, to stay in compliance, we are not really fixing anything, but we are just making it harder for everyone?" Lilla answered, "Yes," adding, "I know that the district will be audited again and I know what they [the state] are going to be looking for. State Ed will look for this [the date on the IEP], so we need to focus on it and get it right." The room erupted after her comment and suddenly one psychologist's voice boomed out of the din, "Let's stop this! None of this follows the spirit of the law!" Lilla directly responded, acknowledging his concern:

> The district is too far off from compliance RIGHT NOW. We can't not focus on compliance details. Don't you know you should be working 24 hours a day, 7 days a week, seeing students and getting all of your paperwork in line?! If you did this, then Sunderville should be in compliance within 3 years! Listen, I've got to be real. Right now, we need to do this [solely focus on compliance] because if there was a special education meeting jail, we would already be in it.

The psychologists were clearly dissatisfied with her reasoning, but they appreciated the humor in her explanation. Lilla also made it clear that although the educators' frustrations mattered to her, their feelings would not change how she and her administrative team operated, because achieving full regulatory compliance with IDEA was their priority. This tension, between compliance and its impact on practice, surfaces a policy implementation paradox that raises questions about whether or not complying with IDEA is actually a path toward achieving equity. It also highlights how the administrative team's insistence on achieving procedural compliance dehumanized the civil rights intent of IDEA. The administrative team satisficed and used IDEA compliance to meet organizational needs, but they did not sufficiently account for how students and educators were negatively affected by the dogged focus on compliance. Compliance inadvertantly became a technical matter, not a substantive matter.

Gerrytown: "Paperwork" Compliance

Roger often told me that each school building and principal in Gerrytown operated on its own accord and that he could not rely upon the superintendent to support his efforts to improve the learning conditions for students with disabilities across the district. Due to this, he said that even though meeting compliance with IDEA was difficult to achieve, he felt it was the only tool he had to ensure that there was some procedural consistency across the district—a form of bounded rationality, because Roger made decisions about compliance that were reactive to his perceived locus of control within a disjointed school system. Roger was very open about this aspect of his workflow, yet he was uncomfortable with how much time and effort he put into ensuring compliance with IDEA was met. This discomfort didn't stop him from focusing on the matter, though.

Roger described his job to me as "all about [the] paperwork" that he needed to complete in order to remain in regulatory compliance. He also pushed his staff to have their paperwork in line and often designed and conducted professional development for his staff that was solely focused on achieving procedural compliance. When I inquired about why he did this, he told me that he had "to design PDs [professional developments]" that started at the "baseline" in order to "get everyone on the same page" and "keep the state off our back," referring to the state auditors who monitor compliance with IDEA in his district. Essentially, Roger strived to use IDEA mandates to unite his staff around a common set of practices. However, he could not speak to how the procedures were enacted in each building. But at least he knew that his staff was "aware" that the procedures had to be followed. This strategy contributed to loose coupling, and it muted the substantive intent of IDEA when the policy was applied in practice.

For example, I observed a professional development session Roger designed for the special education department that illustrated how he prioritized procedural compliance to unite district practices. The professional development (PD) session was 1.5 hours long and had about 50 members of the district staff present. As I sat through the PD, I was astounded by how much time and effort was put toward two goals: (1) directing staff to use specific language to write present levels of performance goals on student IEPs, and (2) ensuring that specific forms for special education referrals were consistently used by all staff. Roger told me before the PD started that these were the two issues the state auditors were monitoring "this year," so he was going to focus on them with his staff.

The meeting began with Roger handing out a stack of papers to everyone in the room with the words "Procedural vs. Substantive: Compliance and Best Practices" written on it. He welcomed everybody to the PD by saying, "Last year was about compliance and what we needed to meet the minimum standards. But this year we are moving toward best practices. Last year we were scraping by and doing things like, 'Oh, the state is not going to look at this so who cares about it now,' but now we have to get into it," referring to the need to ensure compliance with all mandates across the entire district. He added, "last year was nuts, and we busted our butts for compliance," and this year, "we are trying to make things more meaningful and eventually make the IEP a live document." The handouts he gave to his staff had a range of information, from specific directions on how to write positively stated IEP goals to the technical descriptions of federal and state education regulations.

As Roger went through each handout, he explicitly justified its content. For example, when he talked through the handout related to creating positively stated IEP goals, he said, "We didn't just pull these [the positive IEP goals] out of nowhere. It is what the state will be looking for as they come in and do a review, so everyone should follow this." He encouraged his staff to copy the words on the handout into students' IEPs "as is." A district psychologist raised her hand and said the information was helpful and it will make writing IEP goals "a lot easier." The educators in the room chattered with excitement about this handout in particular, because it provided them with specific language they could use to write an IEP goal. It did not help them understand how to meaningfully enact the IEP goal, though.

The PD eventually ended with Roger directing everyone's attention to a large stack of different-colored papers organized on the shelves in the back of the room. When pointing to the shelves, he reminded his staff that the papers were color-coded for a reason. He explained that when a state auditor "comes in and wants to see something in a student's special education file," Roger would know "exactly what color sheet to go to" in the file. He added:

> All of this makes it easier for the state to look for it and also so
> they don't go through our files and find more things needlessly.
> The district is under a focused review and the state is literally
> reviewing every piece of paper that they can go through. . . . If

we don't use the colored forms, we are then inviting the state
[auditors] to sit in on special education meetings and we'll have
state people lurking around checking out how we do things.

He then added, "If the word *must* is in a memo from my office, then you
have to do it to keep the state off our butts. We don't want to lose money
or have state ed sitting with us in these [special education and professional
development] meetings."

Roger took procedural compliance seriously and he wanted his staff
to do the same. This approach to compliance had unintended equity implications, though, because it created conditions where educators in the district, including Roger, could do the "doable job" rather than the "ideal job"
(Bowker & Star, 2000, p. 24) when servicing students with disabilities. This
was most evident in how non-English-speaking parents were included in the
IEP process and in how IEP meetings were conducted.

Managing Language Barriers Through Compliance. Gerrytown has a large
population of non-English-speaking parents and the district does not have
the resources to meet their needs. For instance, the district does not have
a diverse staff or many staff members who speak Spanish or Creole, the
dominant languages in the community. However, through IDEA Gerrytown
School District is legally mandated to provide language services to students,
parents, and guardians whose primary language is not English, and they
have to have access to bilingual related service providers. Because the district does not have these resources, Roger looked to outside consultants to
remedy the district's deficiency. The consultants generally had two roles:
one, facilitate language translation during special education meetings, and
two, report on the academic and social progress of students to non-English-speaking parents and guardians during committee on special education meetings.

The consultants and related service providers that interacted with the
district had little to no relationship with the students or families in the district, and this often negatively affected meetings. For example, when the
district needed a translator for a special education meeting, they utilized a
"language line." The language line was a telephone service that district staff
would call during a meeting and select the language they needed from an
automated menu prompt. Once a language was selected, a human translator would be assigned to the meeting and the district staff would put the
translator on speakerphone. As district staff engaged in conversation during
the meeting, the translator would either translate every word, interrupt and
translate every so often, or would have to be reminded to translate after the
district staff spoke for a long time without pausing. This caused many problems, as information would be mistranslated or ignored and/or an inordinate
amount of time would be spent translating every word stated in the meeting.

During one special education meeting that I attended, which was allocated 45 minutes on Roger's master schedule, the majority of the time was spent waiting in awkward silence because the language line mistakenly brought on a Korean translator when a Creole one was requested. Nearly 30 minutes passed before the correct translator came on the line. The meeting then proceeded with the translator translating every word verbatim to the parents who were in attendance. The constant interruption from the speakerphone left both the district staff and the parents confused, as all forms of communication were lost in translation. And the 15 minutes that remained to discuss the student's needs were mostly spent translating introductions.

Language barriers were also an issue when related service provider consultants attended committee on special education meetings. I sat in on many special education meetings where I observed related service provider consultants reading speech, language, and/or physical therapy reports in very technical and hard to understand language to parents and/or guardians. The reports were often delivered without contextual knowledge about a child and they were very difficult to follow. The consultant would read verbatim a paragraph from the related service report in English to the district staff and then translate the paragraph, verbatim, into the parent and/or guardian's language. The consultants were very clear, to both the district staff and parents, that they were reading the reports verbatim. This resulted in the consultant providing a disjointed and technical report about a student that was difficult to use to support a student's learning and growth.

While these reports were being read, I repeatedly observed parents nodding their heads in agreement without asking many follow-up questions. The district staff acted similarly, partly because the reports were often shared with district staff minutes before a meeting would start, and the staff did not have time to process the reports before a meeting started. However, despite these challenges, the district was in regulatory compliance with IDEA mandates, because a multidisciplinary team was convened to discuss a student's needs, a translator was present, related services were provided, and a parent and/or guardian was in attendance at the meeting.

Efficiency Over Quality and the IEP Meeting. One day I observed several back-to-back IEP annual review meetings at the high school in Gerrytown. I was shadowing the high school psychologist, Katie, as she led these meetings. By 10 a.m., we had already gone through four meetings and we were ahead of schedule by almost 2 hours. This was strange to me because the other special education meetings I had attended in the district were often time-consuming and did not end early. I noted this observation to Katie and she proudly told me, "I like to keep the meetings quick!" Katie was proud of her efficiency and she told me to tell Roger how "good" she was at completing annual reviews "really fast." The social worker and the special education teacher who were also at the meeting looked pleased with her efficiency.

The staff were complying with IDEA in a way that was consistent with how Roger asked them to comply; the right actions were taken to achieve compliance, however the outcomes of those actions were not a central focus.

As we waited for our next meeting to start, a male teacher entered the room. He was the case manager for the white, male, high school senior we were about to have a meeting with and about. The case manager was responsible for monitoring the boy's academic and behavioral reports and he was charged with monitoring his progress toward graduation and completion of his IEP goals. When the case manager sat down at the table we were at, Katie asked, "What's up?" An odd silence followed; the case manager smiled but did not reply. Katie then looked directly at the case manager and asked what type of high school diploma the boy was aspiring to achieve. The case manager said, "I have no idea," and then looked around the table and asked if anyone else knew the answer. One after another, the professionals at the table said that they had "no idea." Katie looked at the case manager again, feigned anger, and said, "You are useless!" She then asked more pointedly, "Shouldn't you know, since you are his case manager?" The case manager laughed and Katie jokingly rolled her eyes at him. She appeared to be more humored by the situation than bothered by it.

The purpose of the IEP meeting suddenly became overshadowed by the chaos occurring in the hall just outside the room we were sitting in. Katie saw a group of students through the door running in the hall and she yelled out to them, "Go to class!" She then looked at all of us and asked, "Why are there kids walking around the halls with four people [security and school aides] at the front door?" No one said anything, so Katie looked at the case manager again and asked, "Is he [the student] going to graduate?" The case manager fumbled through some files and answered, "I dunno." Katie replied, "You suck," and the case manager laughed again. The guidance counselor then asked, "Why are there so many seniors tanking and they think they are going to graduate?" The team at the table kind of laughed, and the special education teacher said, "Well, probably because in years past, people have graduated!" The hallways were still noisy at this point, so the guidance counselor raised her voice to say that she had had a parent ask her, "Why can't my kid play football?" She waited a minute before continuing and then said even louder, "Because your kid isn't passing class!" implying that the parent didn't understand that the child had to pass his classes in order to play sports in the district. This prompted the general education teacher at the table to say, "Parents don't follow through!" Everyone agreed with him.

The guidance counselor then posed another question to the group, "Why can kids pass if they miss 30 classes?" Katie looked at her and answered, "Because there is no attendance policy!" Katie appeared frustrated at this time and asked the guidance counselor what classes the boy was failing. The guidance counselor looked through her papers and said he was failing anatomy. The social worker, who had been mostly silent in the meeting, quipped, "I would fail anatomy." Katie looked around the table and then said, "I am just going to end this kid's meeting because he is not here and no one knows anything." With this, the case manager and the social worker left. However, on his IEP she was able to show that the multidisciplinary team convened to discuss the boy's progress and that his IEP goals would remain as they were.

After the case manager left, Katie closed her computer. I asked her if we were done with the day's meetings and she said, "No." The special education teacher who had been sitting with us the entire meeting looked at her closed computer and asked, "What if something happens in the next meeting that is not recorded in the IEP?" The meeting was supposed to be with a Black female senior. Katie replied, "The girl is a hot f—ing mess" and "nothing will change with her"; "I know the games the girl will play, so the meeting should take only about 10 minutes." The special education teacher agreed with her and they waited for the next meeting to begin.

Katie had already filled out the girl's IEP prior to the meeting. She had determined the outcome of the meeting before it even occurred. This meant that no matter what the professionals in the room said about the girl, she would not be granted any changes to her IEP. By doing this, Katie symbolically showed compliance with IDEA on paper. However, paperwork compliance didn't mean that the girl, or students in Gerrytown more generally, received high-quality educational services. And the way in which Katie and the meeting's participants satisfied around the IEP process made their workflow manageable, but it did not increase educational opportunity and equity for all students. Essentially, the equity implications of their actions were never questioned. Rather, they were taken for granted as sound educational practice, and Roger supported them.

Huntertown: Race, Climate, and Compliance

Huntertown is a very manicured community. The physical layout of the town's center is aesthetically cohesive and invokes a small-town familiarity. It is lined with white picket fences and seasonally decorated lampposts. During fieldwork, I watched the lampposts change from colorful blooming flower baskets to fall cornucopias to carefully placed evergreen wreaths with perfectly taut red bows. The district's offices were folded into the aesthetic appeal of the town, nestled next to an impressive fountain, park, and sprawling athletic fields where students often played field hockey or football after school.

Huntertown is also a primarily white, wealthy, and demographically stable community and school district. The district does not have many Black or Latinx students, and the educators in the district were proud of the cultural "cohesiveness" in the district and community as one elementary school teacher told me. This cohesiveness affected how policies like IDEA were leveraged to support diverse students, and also affected how educators satisficed when complying with IDEA. In particular, I often observed how Black male students classified with a disability in Huntertown were negatively affected by the intersection between local contextual conditions, IDEA compliance, and the process of satisficing; as seen in the case of Xavier, an 8th-grade Black male student in the year of research who had stolen an iPod from the middle school technology room a few months into the school year.

Xavier was one of the approximately 23 Black students classified with a disability in a district that had a total of 40 Black students enrolled across the K–12 system. Cynthia described Xavier as a "high-functioning student," but he had both academic and cognitive delays. He was placed in a self-contained 12:1:1 classroom. This meant that he had 12 peers, one teacher, and one other adult in the room. This type of classroom setting is relatively restrictive on the LRE (least restrictive environment) continuum because the ratio of adults to students is low.

After the iPod was stolen and school-based administrators figured out who had taken it, a special education meeting was called for Xavier. Cynthia told me the purpose of the meeting was to discuss the "iPod incident" and his classroom placement along the LRE continuum. His self-contained teacher had initiated the meeting. The meeting's participants consisted of Cynthia, Xavier's foster grandmother, the school psychologist Xavier worked with, his special education teacher, and myself. In the meeting, I learned that his teacher wanted to recommend Xavier for an out-of-district residential treatment center, a very restrictive environment.

The meeting began with Xavier's teacher, a white woman, explaining what had happened with the iPod. Xavier brought an iPod to school and showed his teacher the device. When he showed her the device, she realized that it was the same one that had gone missing from the technology room. In that conversation she confronted Xavier and tried to get him to admit to stealing it and to "feel bad for taking it." She explicitly told his foster grandmother that she told Xavier he would be assigned a probation officer if proven guilty because the theft was "probation worthy." This scared Xavier and he admitted to her that he took the iPod. As she told the story, she kept reiterating that Xavier "did not feel remorse" and that he was not a "right fit" for her classroom.

Midway through the story, Cynthia interrupted by stating, "For me, this is a bigger issue." The psychologist concurred, adding that she thought Xavier was "asking for help" by actually showing the teacher the iPod. Cynthia pressed the team to ponder what was going on with Xavier that he would steal from the school and specifically from a teacher with whom he had "a good relationship" (the technology room teacher). Cynthia also explicitly stated, "I want to just repeat and make sure we all remember this is confidential," referring to the conversation and content of the meeting.

Throughout the meeting, his teacher continually pushed to have Xavier taken out of her classroom. She recommended that he be considered for an IEP diploma, which would seriously limit his postgraduation options and make future endeavors like employment and college admission more difficult for him. Cynthia did not allow her recommendation to have much discussion time, stating she thought Xavier was "much more capable than an IEP diploma."

Xavier's foster grandmother used Cynthia's pushback against the teacher's repeated recommendation for a more restrictive environment to dissent. She said, "My [grand]son sometimes comes home complaining of 'baby work'" from the teacher's class. His foster grandmother said she tried to tell Xavier that he "has to learn the basics" in order to get to the "harder work," but she did not think he was always academically "challenged" at school. The teacher pushed back and said that he was not capable of more difficult work yet, and the grandmother did not offer more related to this matter.

As the discussion continued, Cynthia and the psychologist decided, together with his foster grandmother's feedback, that Xavier was acting out because he was frustrated with school. The meeting ended with the team deciding to change some of Xavier's classes, giving him more variety and rigor. Before everyone left the table, Cynthia stated that she did not think Xavier had a "serious psychological disorder" and thus it was "not warranted for him" to go to the residential center that the teacher had initially recommended. Cynthia reiterated that an IEP diploma would not be considered. Cynthia, the psychologist, and his foster grandmother also decided that Xavier would benefit from increased counseling services before any other educational placements would be considered.

When the meeting ended, I headed to Cynthia's office to debrief. As she sat down at her desk, she opened an email, gasped, and asked me to read it. The email was from Xavier's teacher, who was just in the meeting with us. It was sent to all high school staff, including custodians, security, and food service staff. The email indicated that Xavier had stolen an iPod, that he should not be given any privileges, and that his every move should be tracked by staff. Cynthia looked at me incredulously and asked, "Didn't you hear me say that everything in the meeting was confidential?" After reading the email, Cynthia sent a response to all building staff reminding them of the confidentiality rights of students with disabilities.

Later in the week, Cynthia met with the teacher who had sent the email, the high school building principal, and the district superintendent to speak about the email. The superintendent was not sympathetic to Cynthia's viewpoint, that the email was harmful to the student. She told Cynthia that "the matter was a building issue" and it was up to the high school principal to decide how it would be handled. The high school principal said she knew about the email prior to it being sent to district staff and she saw "nothing wrong with it." Cynthia tried to tell the high school principal that the email "put a bull's eye on the kid [Xavier]" to fail, yet the principal again said she did not "see an issue" with the email.

In fact, the principal told Cynthia that she thought the email resulted in positive outcomes because a custodian and a security guard had already reported Xavier walking the halls without permission. The building principal also said Xavier "reportedly punched" a child outside of the school and that a girl reported to the high school principal that she did not want to leave school because she was "scared of him [Xavier]." All of the complaints happened within 2 days of the initial email being sent to the staff.

In summary, Xavier had stolen an iPod, which he showed to his teacher, claiming it was his. Cynthia and the psychologist interpreted this action as a "cry for help" and they wanted to offer him more counseling services through IDEA. Xavier's foster grandmother advocated for her grandson, but her requests never materialized beyond the confines of the meeting. Xavier did not have the chance to use the extra services that were discussed in the meeting because of the email the teacher sent to school staff. And, after the meeting occurred, Xavier was put in a vulnerable situation that resulted in a suspension from school.

Essentially, the culture and climate of Huntertown did not adequately support Xavier. There were subtle yet clear moments when Xavier and his family were systematically denied the opportunity to fully leverage the benefits of IDEA. The context and climate of Huntertown ensured that Xavier was systematically denied the opportunity to rectify his actions, and a series of decisions made by the administrative and teaching staff put him in a more vulnerable position when being disciplined. And, regardless of the fact that Cynthia tried to use the special education process to help Xavier prior to his suspension, her attempts were thwarted by a district climate that appeared unwilling to be sympathetic to Xavier's needs. In the end, though, the district was in compliance with IDEA because a multidisciplinary team was convened to discuss Xavier's case and more services were offered to help him.

THE LIMITS OF IDEA AND COMPLIANCE

Although the civil rights movement influenced the development and eventual passage of IDEA, the legislation has maintained a procedural focus to ensure that civil rights outcomes are realized for students with disabilities in schools. This has resulted in a legislative climate that has pushed some school districts, like Sunderville and Gerrytown, to prioritize compliance with IDEA in a manner that does not honor the substantive intent of the legislation. The procedural focus of IDEA has also generated an environment where educators can symbolically comply with IDEA and satisfice in a way that is responsive to their local sociocultural context. This allows for IDEA to be applied to practice in a way that does not challenge biases or norms that may systematically disadvantage some students over others. This was clearly evident in Huntertown, where the climate and culture of the school district were relatively unresponsive to Xavier's needs. Collectively, the stories about compliance with IDEA coming from Sunderville, Gerrytown, and Huntertown expose some of the broader limitations associated with IDEA implementation because, while IDEA is noble in its intent to provide a free appropriate public education to all students, the enforcement structure behind the legislation is not strong enough to ensure that equal educational opportunity and access are provided to all students and that local contextual factors do not thwart its legislative intent.

For instance, Wakelin (2008) identifies three intertwining factors that lead to difficulties in substantively enforcing IDEA in practice. They exist at the federal, state, and parental level (20 U.S.C. §§ 1415–1416 [2000 & Supp. IV 2004]). At the federal level, Wakelin (2008) identifies five requirements that states must fulfill in order to receive and qualify for IDEA funding from the federal government:

1. SEAs must have a policy ensuring that all children with disabilities between the ages of 3 to 21 have a right to FAPE;
2. SEAs must have a plan to spend money from the Office of Special Education Programs (OSEP) in a way that is consistent with the legislative intent of IDEA;
3. SEAs must create plans that include procedural safeguards for parents;
4. SEAs and LEAs must ensure that all children are educated in the least restrictive environment; and
5. SEAs and LEAs must use testing and evaluation materials that are racially and/or culturally nondiscriminatory.

If a state does not meet these requirements, the federal government can withhold IDEA funds and resources. However, even though nearly every state is in some form of noncompliance with IDEA, the Office of Special Education Programs (OSEP) has rarely withheld funds from a state (Wakelin, 2008).

At the state level, SEAs must ensure that a free appropriate public education (FAPE) is provided to all students in their jurisdiction and that educational services are provided to students who have been evaluated as having a disability. Federal monitoring of this is spotty, at best, because SEAs cannot logistically monitor and verify all LEA actions related to compliance with IDEA. SEAs often take evidence of compliance, via documentation and LEA compliance reports, as sufficient proof that IDEA has been substantively and appropriately applied to practice (Wakelin, 2008).

Lastly, parents are given a central role in the administration of IDEA. According to Wakelin's (2008) analysis of IDEA's effectiveness, and citing a report by the National Council for Disability, Wakelin highlights how the report found "that due to twenty-five years of federal non-enforcement, parental advocacy is the main enforcement mechanism of the IDEA" (p. 273). This is highly problematic, because substantive application of IDEA to practice is thus contingent upon parental social, economic, and cultural capital and parents' access to information that allows them to successfully advocate for their child(ren) within schools. Thus, the enforcement gaps that exist at the federal, state, and parental level generate many spaces and places where policy-to-practice gaps manifest that do not adequately protect all students from discriminatory practices because evidence of compliance with IDEA's procedural protections is sufficient to ensure civil rights outcomes, even though high-quality educational opportunities are not provided to *all* learners, as evidenced in the compliance practices of Sunderville, Gerrytown, and Huntertown.

CHAPTER 2

Educational Opportunity and Racial Inequities in Special Education

Research has shown that Black and Native American students are overclassified and/or placed in special education (Donovan & Cross, 2002; Losen & Orfield, 2002; U.S. Department of Education, 2009), and/or suspended from school (Losen, 2014), while English language learners (ELLs) have regionally varying patterns of overrepresentation (Artiles, Rueda, Salazar, & Higareda, 2005; Samson & Lesaux, 2009; Sullivan, 2011). In addition, Black, Native American, and Latinx students are underrepresented in gifted-and-talented programs (Ford 1998; Ford, Scott, Moore, & Amos, 2013; Harris & Ford, 1999). These differential patterns of educational access and opportunity are the result of complex factors that are not solely linked to individual learning capacities (e.g., Skiba et al., 2008; Waitoller, Artiles, & Cheney, 2010).

For example, research on disproportionality has shown that culturally, racially, ethnically, and linguistically diverse students are often referred to special education without sufficient exposure to high-quality educational interventions that support their learning (Harry & Klingner, 2014; National Research Council, 2002). Students of color are often placed in special education programs that provide limited access to rigorous curriculum and to academically advanced peers (Donovan & Cross, 2002; Harry & Klingner, 2014) and once a child, often a student of color, is placed in special education, there is little movement out of it (Harry & Klingner, 2014). In addition, referrals to and placement into special education—as well as the labels given to students with disabilities—can be highly subjective (Harry & Klingner, 2014; Maheady, Towne, Algozzine, Mercer, & Ysseldyke, 1983), and the methods used in educational practice to assess and teach students with disabilities are often unscientific and based on the day-to-day decisions of school personnel (Harry & Anderson, 1994; Harry & Klingner, 2014). Lastly, Mehan, Hertweck, and Meihls (1986) found that student identities and abilities are created and rigidly defined in special education meetings where educators view past institutional and anecdotal records as evidence of disability rather than evaluating students' current performance. This is particularly consequential for Black students, as they are consistently classified and tracked into lower-quality programs at an earlier age than their school-aged peers (Coutinho, Oswald, Best, & Forness, 2002; Oakes, 2005; Tyson, 2011).

The long-term effects of special education placement are consequential because graduation rates from special education are often low and limit future educational attainment and occupational opportunities (Wells, Sandefur, & Hogan, 2003). In addition, Rutherford, Bullis, Anderson, and Griller-Clark (2002) found that students with disabilities are disproportionately represented in the correctional system and that youth classified in the high-incidence disability categories are four times more likely to enter the correctional system than their nonclassified peers (Rutherford et al., 2002). Complicating the matter is that the disproportionate number of Black males classified with a disability may relate to their high numbers in the criminal justice system and potentially contribute to the school-to-prison pipeline (Kim, Losen, & Hewitt, 2010). These long-term patterns of inequality and injustice are not related to student deficits, but rather are the result of educational opportunity gaps that have systematically denied students of color, particularly Native American, Black, and Latinx students labeled with a disability, access to high-quality educational interventions and services.

EDUCATIONAL OPPORTUNITY GAPS AND DISPROPORTIONALITY

Often, educational inequalities are described through the language of the achievement gap, which is focused on highlighting educational disparities that manifest via individual academic test scores. This framework for understanding educational inequality is embedded in a deficit and individualized framework because it directly links educational disparities to individual learning capacities. However, recent research has reframed the conversation on educational inequality to consider how schools and society more generally do, or do not, provide students with adequate opportunities to learn, which in turn influences academic outcomes and manifests in consequential educational opportunity gaps (e.g., Boykin & Noguera, 2011; Gorski, 2015; Milner, 2010).

Educational opportunity gaps are the result of both structural and interactional components that negatively impact student outcomes. For example, Welner and Carter (2013), in their work on educational inequality, state that educational opportunity gaps are the result of "deficiencies in the foundational components of societies, schools, and communities that produce significant differences in educational—and ultimately socioeconomic—outcomes" for students (p. 3). Educational opportunity gaps are also related to prejudices, racism, classism, and other forms of biases that influence how resources are allocated across and within schools (e.g., Carter & Welner, 2013; Darling-Hammond, 2004). Carter (2013) adds that educational opportunity gaps are exacerbated when educators struggle to "comprehend the social realities, cultural resources, and understandings of Black, Latino, Native American, and other nondominant groups" (p. 147) because these belief systems contribute to cultural dissonance and misunderstandings between educators and students of color that fuel low expectations and misunderstandings of student ability (e.g., Gay, 2010; Delpit, 2006; Harry, Allen, & McLaughlin, 1995; Harry & Klingner, 2014; Ladson-Billings, 1995a, 1995b, 2001; Mehan, 1992; Oakes, 2005; Pollock, 2004). These belief systems are often encased within colorblind and race-neutral frameworks that do not explicitly recognize racial inequalities. And, compounding the issue, multiple researchers have found that educators' belief systems about diverse students, particularly Black and Latinx students, are often subconsciously applied to students regardless of how they are presenting themselves, which in turn negatively impacts student achievement (e.g., Elhoweris, Mutua, Alsheikh, & Holloway, 2005; Irvine, 1992; Peterson et al., 2011; Tobias, Cole, Zibrin, & Bodlakova, 1982; Van Houtte, 2011). Therefore, differential academic achievement patterns are not solely the result of student deficits or limited learning capacities; rather, they are related to structural inequalities and interactional factors that negatively impact student achievement and contribute to inequities like disproportionality.

Structural and Interactional Opportunity Gaps in Suburban Contexts

Racial inequities and educational opportunity gaps—whether they are related to classification, placement, and/or discipline—are more likely to manifest within diverse social contexts, as numerous studies have shown that disproportionate outcomes are related to the sociodemographic context of schools and districts (e.g., Beck & Muschkin, 2012; Martinez, McMahon, & Treger, 2016; Oswald, Coutinho, & Best, 2002; Oswald, Coutinho, Best, & Singh, 1999; Skiba, Poloni-Staudinger, Simmons, Renae Feggins-Azziz, & Chung, 2005; Skiba et al., 2014; Sullivan, Klingbeil, & Van Norman, 2013). The relationship between sociodemographic changes and racial inequities in special education is especially consequential in suburban school districts because suburban school districts are shifting away from being primarily white neighborhoods to being more diverse ones (e.g., Frey, 2011; Fry, 2009). However, as suburban school districts are demographically shifting they are also becoming increasingly segregated throughout the process of change (Frankenberg & Orfield, 2012).

For instance, Wells et al. (2012), in their work on suburban segregation and migration, cite Adelman (2005) and point out that "there is strong evidence that African Americans, in particular, remain highly segregated in both urban *and* suburban contexts." The authors also note that "black suburbanization is rarely accompanied by racial integration, and that even middle-class African Americans remain highly segregated" (p. 128) in suburban contexts. However, despite these persistent patterns of racial housing segregation, schools do initially integrate and they are often the first sites where increased community diversity is experienced (Orfield, 2002). This underscores how important it is for school systems and educators to be prepared to teach all students, but they are often not prepared to do so, as there are very few policies that support suburban educators in contending with demographic shifts, and there is very little municipal and civil rights coordination to prevent racial and economic residential segregation from occurring in suburban contexts (Frankenberg & Orfield, 2012).

The issues associated with suburban demographic change and schools are consequential on student outcomes because educational opportunity gaps and disproportionate outcomes are associated with the historical legacy of segregation, educational tracking, and the failed racial integration of schools across the United States. For example, using a racial dissimilarity index measuring a community's level of segregation, Eitle (2002) found that racial segregation contributes to the disproportionate representation of Black students in mentally retarded (now intellectual disability) programs. Segregation also infiltrates within-school processes by tracking students, which in its most extreme form manifests as a special education placement. Tyson (2011) argues that racialized tracking "is essentially segregation" when the tracks have racial characteristics, highlighting a "deep irony in the fact that the institution that is supposed to level social differences and to render background characteristics unimportant, instead more often openly reinforces and exacerbates those differences" (p. 28). Racialized tracking within schools also reflects broader patterns of racial and class stratification that exists across schools and within society (Oakes, 2005). Even more problematic, segregation generates and reinforces negative stereotypes about different groups of students (Wells, 2009), which is related to the misperceptions and cultural dissonance that contribute to educational issues such as disproportionality in special education.

Educational opportunity gaps are also sustained when race-neutral and/or colorblind frameworks guide educational practice. Frankenberg and Orfield (2012) found that in demographically changing suburban school districts educators use colorblind mindsets to address issues of diversity. They argue that suburban educators rely on standards-based educational policies, which do not purposefully engage with the racial and class inequities that may be present in local contexts, to address educational issues. This approach is problematic because when social contexts diversify colorblind mindsets, deficit thinking, and culturally biased assumptions about students influence how educational services are delivered to students and ultimately determine who is deemed deserving of those educational services (e.g., Cooper, 2009; Evans, 2007; Holme, Diem, & Welton, 2014; Lewis, 2001; Murrillo, 2002). And, when colorblindness is used as a default frame to administer educational assessments, interventions, and evaluations to students who are perceived as having cognitive and/or behavior problems, disproportionality is rationalized (e.g., Annamma, Connor, & Ferri, 2013; Artiles, 2009; Connor, Ferri, & Anamma, 2016; Leonardo & Broderick, 2011).

This is because a colorblind and race-neutral framework downplays the salience of race, racial inequality, and the impact of potentially racist practices (Bonilla-Silva, 1997, 2015, 2017; Doane, 2017) on educational outcomes. It also allows for racial inequities to be attributed to student characteristics rather than to educators' beliefs and biases, social norms, social contexts, social systems, and social structures.

For example, Neal, McCray, Webb-Johnson, and Bridgest (2003) found that white teachers perceive Black children as being more fearful than other students when walking and talking, and they relate this behavior to lower academic achievement. Skiba et al. (2006) found that white teachers were aware that they did not feel prepared to work with racially, culturally, ethnically, and linguistically diverse students' behaviors and that they perceived special education as an appropriate placement for students they did not understand. Vavrus and Cole (2002) found that when Black students questioned authority or spoke loudly, they were referred for disciplinary action more often than white students. And Gregory and Weinstein (2008) found that Black students were referred more often than other students for disciplinary action when their behaviors were labeled with a subjective infraction such as being "defiant" or "noncompliant" with school rules and procedures. This line of research shows that racialized outcomes manifest even when educators do not explicitly discriminate or intend to deny educational opportunities to racially, culturally, ethnically, and linguistically diverse students. This has equity implications because the impact of educators' belief systems, coupled with social contextual conditions and colorblind sentiments, systematically deny educational opportunity to diverse learners.

While in the field, I repeatedly observed some students, mostly Black and Latinx males, regularly receiving lower-quality educational services and interventions than other students. The disparate provision of educational resources to diverse students, which I observed in all three districts, was often wrapped in colorblind and race-neutral talk that failed to acknowledge how race influenced educators' decisionmaking processes and how race shaped educators' capacity and willingness to relate to diverse students. This "colormute" (Pollock, 2009) talk had negative impacts on student outcomes, because it did not hold educators accountable for the aggregate impacts of their micro-actions on student outcomes.

The intersection between the local community context and school system impacted student outcomes as well. This is because the differential provision of educational opportunities to students in suburban communities like Huntertown, Sunderville, and Gerrytown is related to broader social forces that are associated with the historical migration of white, Black, and Latinx families in and out of suburbs in the United States. These trends of demographic change, associated with persistent racial segregation and failed integration, impact schools and districts as there are both "social" and "symbolic" boundaries (Wells et al., 2012) that affect how education is locally understood and how educational resources are allocated within local communities, which collectively lead to educational opportunity gaps. Symbolic boundaries mark such things as networks of power and privilege that influence how educational resources are distributed within local contexts. Social boundaries justify the unequal distribution of these resources. Wells et al. (2012) distinguish between the two concepts by stating that "social boundaries serve to perpetuate unequal material conditions across district lines and thus help to legitimize the symbolic boundaries woven into the identities of 'place' within the field of education" (p. 132). In other words, local norms, ways of being, and networks of power and privilege legitimize social boundaries, which in turn strengthen symbolic boundaries. Thus, when a community that is relatively demographically stable and homogenous like Huntertown, diversifying like Sunderville, and/or segregated like Gerrytown, is faced with racial inequalities like disproportionality, the local history and community context are equally implicated in the generation of racial inequities like disproportionality, as are the educators who are working within those contexts. This is because the demographic and contextual conditions of the community create unspoken parameters that shape who gets what educational services and who deserves those educational services, and that often manifest in disparate racialized outcomes.

For instance, the racial homogeneity of Huntertown School District sustained strong social norms that excluded and denied educational opportunities to students of color, particularly Black males. In Sunderville, educators struggled to adjust to the diversifying community context and this negatively impacted how they related to and serviced diverse students. In Gerrytown, the historical legacy of racial and economic segregation in the community and school district affected the connections educators had with students and families. And, collectively across all three districts, the demographic shifts and patterns of racial and economic segregation influenced how educational opportunities and resources were distributed to diverse students, which ultimately contributed to the persistence of racial inequities in the local context.

Huntertown: Missed Educational Opportunities

In Huntertown, I met a student, Claude, whose story illustrates how both structural and interactional educational opportunity gaps coalesced, despite the best intentions of educators, to deny him consistent access to high-quality educational services. Claude was a tall Black 7th-grader attending Huntertown School District in the year of research. His IEP indicated that in kindergarten he had been classified as speech and language impaired (SLI) after having been identified in preschool as being "aggressive" and "inappropriate with kids." He exited in and out of the formal school system in the early grades and did not have regular contact with his parents. His foster grandparents were raising him.

By the 2nd grade, Claude's school-based files indicated that his teachers were confused as to why he had been classified as SLI, so his classification was changed to learning disabled (LD) in 3rd grade. In the research year, his files indicated he was unable to read and he was given assistive technology, in the form of a reading pen through IDEA funds, to help him access and read complex texts. In addition, a bus was secured to help him get to school.

I first heard about Claude in a meeting that I was attending with the high school principal who oversaw grades 7–12 in the district. I did not know Claude's name yet, but I noticed that out of approximately 10 students being discussed in the meeting, two were not spoken of very highly and one was Claude. Claude and his family were being criticized for receiving bus services while his foster grandmother simultaneously wanted him to be mainstreamed into general education classes. The apparent incongruity between the push for mainstreaming and the concern that Claude could not get to school on his own caused laughter and frustration among the meeting's participants. After that meeting, I had my ears tuned into hearing more about Claude and I often heard staff speak about him while I was sitting in Cynthia's office.

For example, one day when I was sitting in Cynthia's office, she realized she didn't have information about whether or not Claude attended summer school prior to the 2011–2012 school year. Apparently, he had been slated to attend summer school but never went. As Cynthia tried to figure out if he had attended summer school or not, she yelled to her secretary through her office door, "Why didn't he go to summer school?" Her secretary replied that summer school had never been finalized "because of travel training issues," which were associated with Claude's foster grandmother wanting to secure a bus for him to take to school and the district's reluctance to provide one. It seemed as though because Claude was not guaranteed bus services, he missed the opportunity to attend summer school. Cynthia seemed unconcerned about this, shrugged her shoulders, and moved on to her next task, seemingly satisfied with her secretary's response and her ability to click "no" on the computer indicating that Claude had not attended summer school. Throughout my fieldwork, I noticed that overlooked details and missed educational opportunities, like the one described here, traveled with Claude despite the fact that Claude had a case manager who was his "school-based advocate."

Every child in the Huntertown School District classified with a disability had a case manager. Claude's was Sally, the high school director of special education. She would often come to Cynthia's office and chat informally about students, curriculum, and/or district matters. One day, Sally came to Cynthia's office to speak about several students who were concerning her. One of them was Claude.

Sally said that Claude was "really struggling" in his classes, adding that he was not a "bad kid," but that he was avoiding schoolwork. Cynthia told Sally that she thought Claude would benefit from a specific reading intervention she introduced to her staff in the beginning of the school year, the Wilson Reading Program. When Cynthia mentioned the Wilson Reading Program, Sally groaned and said she would give Claude the program "if I have to." Cynthia wanted her staff to use the Wilson Reading Program because it fulfilled some of the state's requirements for multi-tiered systems and supports (MTSS) to support struggling learners. However, the staff in Huntertown did not want to receive training in the program.

When Cynthia shared with her staff that she wanted them to attend professional development workshops related to the Wilson Reading Program in late September, the teaching staff united, got the teachers' union's backing, and refused to be trained in the program. I reached out to Sally shortly after the staff meeting in September and inquired about why the staff did not want to attend the trainings related to the Wilson Reading Program. Sally told me the teachers in the district did not see "much value" in the program because it was time-consuming and would not "affect many students." After asking around a bit, I found out that the program's services would be primarily used for a few Black students who were included in the district's citation for disproportionality. In my conversation with Sally, she also told me that the training was "put on" teachers in the beginning of the school year when there were already numerous work demands. Basically, she told me there was "very little incentive" to do it, and it was not until later on in the school year, when a white parent with connections to the school board needed Wilson services, that a few staff members were trained in the program.

When Sally refused Cynthia's suggestion for the Wilson Reading Program to help Claude, Cynthia asked Sally if Claude would benefit from using a laptop. Cynthia often recommended assistive technology to students in the district. Sally immediately responded, "I would be worried if the laptop went home that it might not come back," and that "maybe Claude would benefit from vocational education." Cynthia immediately dismissed the recommendation for vocational education because it would limit his capacity to receive a high school diploma and possibly attend college. Sally did not want to spend time discussing how something like a laptop or a reading intervention might help Claude. Instead, she wanted to push him to a more restrictive environment. At the end of the meeting with Sally, Cynthia encouraged her to tell Claude to visit her in her office so she could see what was going on with him.

I soon realized that Sally wasn't the only one who didn't want to directly help Claude. One teacher in particular, Rhonda, often visited Cynthia's office. When she visited she would informally check in about students and she often spoke about Claude. One day, during one of these informal meetings with Cynthia, Rhonda said she was "crying with Claude" because he was struggling in her class. She lamented that he could not read and that she was trying to figure out how to help him. Cynthia asked if he was using his reading pen, which she had secured for him with IDEA funds and was written into his IEP, and she also asked Rhonda if a laptop would help him. Before Cynthia could finish her sentence, Rhonda cried out, "He just can't learn!" He "will waste the technology and use it to play and not to learn." Rhonda looked frustrated, threw her hands up in the air, and asked Cynthia if Claude could go to a more restrictive environment. Cynthia said that was not an option. Again, it seemed as if another educator was unwilling to provide the time and energy needed to possibly assist Claude in his reading.

Cynthia used Rhonda's suggestion for a more restrictive learning environment to ask if Claude would benefit from the Wilson Reading Program. Rhonda replied, "In confidence, just to give you a heads-up, no one wants to be trained in that program." I was doing some writing in the corner of Cynthia's office when she said this and Rhonda noticed as she continued to speak about Claude. She looked at me and said, "Next time I will filter myself," implying that she was about to say something about Claude that was inappropriate, and then proceeded to say that if she were going to give Claude the reading intervention or "even consider it, he would need to shower first." She asked Cynthia, "Have you seen his nails? They have so much dirt under them and he stinks!" She again looked at me and told me she would filter herself around me the next time and laughed. The disparaging tone proceeded for a while until the conversation ended with Cynthia suggesting that a special education meeting be convened for Claude so that the staff could discuss some of the issues he was facing. Rhonda used racially coded language about Claude that was insensitive and judgmental. She did not want to deal with Claude and she made that clear during nearly every visit she made to Cynthia's office.

A few weeks later, Sally did hold an IEP meeting to discuss Claude's case with his foster grandmother. During the meeting there was no record of or talk about the reading intervention or his reading issues. His IEP file remained mostly static. He would continue to use the reading pen, but he would no longer receive travel training despite his foster grandmother's objection to discontinuing it. The IEP process was not leveraged to assist Claude; instead, services were stripped from his IEP and he was left in the same spot as before the meeting, struggling to read, and without a real plan to help him.

In summary, both structural and interactional educational opportunity gaps manifested and were sustained through micro-decisions made by the educators surrounding Claude, who in the aggregate systematically denied him access to high-quality educational interventions and services. For instance, although Sally and Rhonda both knew that Claude was struggling in school, they were not willing to give him the extra time and attention he needed to succeed. Rather, a reading pen was deemed sufficient for meeting his educational needs, and his bathing patterns were sufficient rationale for why his teacher, Rhonda, would not help him further. In addition, his lack of attendance at summer school was regarded as a relatively inconsequential fact. And his caseworker Sally did not advocate for him to receive the benefits of the Wilson Reading Program, which could have potentially helped his reading skills. In addition, despite his foster grandmother's concern over the bus, bus services were discontinued during his IEP meeting and he was given almost exactly the same educational services that he was receiving prior to both Sally and Rhonda coming to Cynthia with concerns about his performance in school. Lastly, although Claude's race was never directly addressed in the interactions described in this ethnographic moment, race played a pivotal role in how educational opportunities were either afforded him or not. While the educators in Huntertown did not explicitly acknowledge that Claude is a Black student classified with a disability in a predominantly white school district with a history of racial inequities in special education, they did make professional decisions that systematically denied Claude crucial opportunities to learn. This had consequences that were racialized, because, as Burke (2017) argues, colorblindness is not just a belief system; it is a belief system that organizes resources, and thus can sustain racial inequities.

Once, while Cynthia was in a particularly reflective mood, sitting in her office, she seemed to realize this fact when she pointed to a picture of a watercolor painting of an elephant hanging on her wall that Claude had painted. While looking at it she said, "Maybe it is a little racist that we are spending so much time securing an iPad2 [for a white boy whose parents were threatening litigation through IDEA] and not helping him [Claude] learn to read," pointing to the elephant he created. Cynthia paused and added, "We [the district] spend so much time trying to secure resources for kids who don't really need them. I think I'm paid to get the parents what they want and not to get the kids what they really need." After this statement, she returned to the paperwork she was filtering through on her desk. Cynthia's comment was profound in the context of Huntertown, yet she seemed to shrug it off just as fast as she had said it. She had identified how the lack of time and attention given to Claude and his needs were in stark contrast to her and her staff's efforts to secure resources for more economically privileged and often white students in the district. Cynthia knew something wasn't right, but she seemed to be unable to realign resources to address what she felt might be wrong.

Sunderville: Dissonance and Discipline in Shifting Contexts

The local community context of Sunderville also affected disproportionality, but in a different way from in Huntertown. In Huntertown, the social cohesion and strong norms operating in the district marginalized students of color and systematically denied the equitable provision of educational resources to all students. In Sunderville, the shifting community context forced both structural and interactional opportunity gaps to collide in schools and classrooms on a daily basis. These collisions generated tensions between educators and students. The educators in the district tried to control these tensions, but they could not, and the tensions often contributed to problems with student safety, tolerance, and disproportionate disciplinary outcomes.

Community Tensions. Although not a rural community, Sunderville stretches across large expanses of winding roads that cut through forests and stands of trees. Each school building in the district mirrors the landscape: They are large, sprawling, and have many hallways that are difficult to navigate. Marc Sown, who had been working in the district for 3 years, would often become lost as we rushed through the buildings when I visited. Once, when I asked Marc's secretary for a map of the high school, the building in which Marc and Lilla's office was housed, she told me, "It's [the map] useless. I can't even figure it out." The sense of inertia I felt when walking through the halls was paradoxically paired with close monitoring of all student, staff, and visitor actions.

One district employee explained to me that most of the buildings in the district were built to be a "purposeful panopticon" on both the inside and outside in order to ensure all students and visitors could be monitored. Whether this was true or not, it felt real. For example, on the outside, the district's schools were nestled into pastoral landscapes peppered with dozens of people wearing bright neon-green jackets with "SECURITY" written in capital letters on their backs. The "green jackets," as they were called, were always the first ones to greet me and any other visitor, student, or staff member coming to the district. Internally, high school students had an ID card with a microchip, which monitored their movement in and out of school buildings. Elementary building entrances were manned with "green jackets" who escorted visitors through the halls. And, almost every hallway in every school in the district had at least one hallway monitor and security guard standing watch.

When I questioned Marc about the tight monitoring of staff, students, and visitors in the district, he told me it was related to a series of hate and bias crimes that had occurred on district grounds over the past few years. These crimes had been frequently recorded by local media sources and they concerned the district's leadership team and staff. The district's superintendent, Dr. Lovene, wanted the district to have a more positive public reputation, so he pushed for each school to maintain close observation of every person entering, exiting, and interacting with district staff and/or students.

The district's problems with tolerance and student safety were a mirror to broader community issues. I observed that Sunderville was "divided and split in two by a railroad track," as one district employee described. Another told me, "one side of the track has old summer homes and estates," while the other side is known for its "'Sunderville trash' or white trash, drugs, and poor people." A building administrator expressed that the estate side of town was "different [because] there's more money over there, more involvement with parents," and, "aesthetically, it's a prettier place, it's a nicer place." The administrator added that the other side of the tracks was known for "its crime and drug issues." The economic segregation in the community was exacerbated by the community's recent demographic shifts. A middle school building administrator shared his thoughts on how the community dealt with the growing diversity in Sunderville and the school district. His statement shows how the racial and class tensions brewing in the community infiltrated the district's schools:

> You know, my secretary, all my secretaries here, who grew up here, their kids grew up here, [they] still take pride here. They welcome the diversity [in Sunderville], and then there's the older generations that are . . . they don't take pride. They take pride in maybe that they've been here for a long time, but I have to ask them, "What have you done to make it [Sunderville] better? What do you do? You just complain. You just say, 'These poor people, these Black people, are ruining everything.'" . . . You know, on top of that, we also have the highest concentration of ex-offenders [in the poorer section of Sunderville]. . . . So these people come out of jail and they get thrown into an already poor housing area, and that throws a wrench into things too. Everybody's cracking on us. . . . It's a Bermuda Triangle over there [by the housing area]. . . . So, as a whole, I think we have different layers here in this large community. We have the older generation that really takes pride in it, that are embracing the diversity. . . . We have the older generations that just blame everybody and then you have the transient population and minorities. . . . The generations that have been here are now blaming all the problems on the minorities, even though the problems were already here. . . . It's a bizarre demographic going on down here. It's a Bermuda Triangle, I tell you.

He described how residents and educators tried to understand and accept the racial and socioeconomic diversity of Sunderville through various lenses. According to his account, some people viewed the changes as a positive thing, while others saw it to be a negative thing. However, no matter how adults made sense of the "Bermuda Triangle" that is Sunderville, the sociodemographic changes greatly affected the climate and culture of Sunderville's schools and impacted students.

Student Impact. The demographic shifts occurring in the community and the tensions that resulted from these shifts had profound impacts on students and educators in the district. I clearly observed how the shifting demographic context interacted with disproportionate outcomes in discipline during my attendance in a "Boys Group." The group was comprised of approximately eight young men of color, particularly Black and Latinx males, and was led by Chris, a high school guidance counselor. The first day I attended the Boys Group, it became crystal clear to me just how consequential the educational opportunity gaps associated with the social context and climate of Sunderville School District were for the young Black and Latinx men attending the group.

The day began with Chris and me in his office. While we waited for the group of eight "at-risk" Black and Latino young men Chris had worked with for the past 2 years to arrive, he told me that when he first met with the group, he realized that most of the boys had been suspended for being "insubordinate," yet few knew what the word meant. Chris said he felt like his "first responsibility" was to teach them about the discipline system in the school so they would not be suspended again. He told me he liked to "give the boys the tools [needed] to de-escalate the moments where they can get into arguments with teachers and then get suspended or in trouble." Shortly after he said this, the boys came into Chris's office.

When the boys entered the room, they quickly sat down and began immediately to talk about the issues on their minds. The meeting started with a young man, Flint, telling the group he was hungry. He had thrown out his lunch because, as he told the group, Mrs. Logan, the high school assistant principal, said, "I couldn't have it [lunch] now, and I didn't want to start anything because she got like five security guards around me. She told me if I got lunch now she could get my education thrown out the window! Can someone just take your education away!?!?" He looked incredulously at Chris when he said this while another student at the table, Billy, said, "Yeah! I always get that! People always saying I'm not going to graduate!" Jared, another boy in the room, added, "Can someone really say that [that they can take your education away]? I mean, man, I got suspended once for just looking mad. It was crazy!" Simon, who had been very quiet during the exchange, said, "That is why I am out [on his way to graduation] and not looking back." Billy added, "Yeah, that's why you got to work hard. I don't like hard work but I just do it now so I can get out of here [the high school]." All the boys nodded in agreement with the statements being tossed around the room.

Suddenly Jared laughed and said, "Yeah, that is so stupid [referring to the lunch story]. We get in trouble for nothing! That is why when the school mails my [disciplinary] referrals to the house my ma just looks at them and laughs and throws them away!" Flint added, "We need a jury and lawyers!" But Billy interjected, "Well, life is not fair and that is what school prepares us for. It prepares us for life."

With Billy's comment, Chris decided to take over the conversation. He stated, "You can either be reactive or proactive in a situation where you are treated unfairly." Flint responded by again referring to his interaction with Mrs. Logan in the lunchroom: "Yeah, that is what I did. I didn't do anything even though I wanted to punch her because she was treating me so badly."

He went on to add that Mrs. Logan had told him, "Cameras are always watching you" and "I have my eye on you and I don't care if you tell Chris that!" Flint went on, "But I was like, 'What?! Why do you watch me and ignore all the drug dealing going on?' I didn't say that, but I thought it." Jared then said, "This school is crazy! But you can't treat disrespect with disrespect," and "Mrs. Logan is always yelling at us even when we are right next to her!" The entire table of boys laughed in agreement.

As they were talking, Chris looked at me and said, "Sometimes the same school staff comes up in this room and it's hard to know what to do about that," referring to Mrs. Logan. He added, "I only have 45 minutes with the boys," so he planned to "let this session go organically." He pointed to Simon, who had spoken the least, and told him to tell me his story.

Simon was very quiet and had his hoodie (sweatshirt) pulled over his head when he started to speak:

> The other day I ate a ham sandwich, and it made me real sick. I knew it was bad when I picked it up, but I was so hungry. I threw up in the bathroom and was trying to go back to class but couldn't make it because I felt so sick. I had to sit down. I just had to. So I sat on the stairs in the hallway with my head in my hands, and I couldn't move, and a teacher came up to me and told me I had to move. I couldn't move and I don't know why the teacher didn't realize that I was sick. I tried to tell him I didn't feel good and just needed a minute, but the teacher wouldn't listen and started to get mad at me for not moving. The teacher started saying he was going to call security, and I told him to do it because I couldn't move because I didn't feel good. We started going at it. I cursed and I actually threw up in the stairway in front of the teacher, but I was still suspended for not being where I was supposed to be.

Chris told me Simon had more than 120 discipline referrals per school year until this group, the Boys Group, was formed. Since then, Simon had not had one referral or suspension until this event, which had happened at the end of May. The "ham sandwich incident was the first time all year [Simon had been disciplined], and he was given 7 days of out-of-school suspension." Simon looked up at me when Chris said this and added, "I didn't feel like I was even treated like a person. I still don't understand how or why that happened." Chris noted Simon's suspension had been labeled as "major insubordination."

The climate of the room felt very heavy after Simon's story. A period of silence was broken by Flint: "Yeah, I hate this school because sometimes they disrespect me so much that I feel like I am an animal. They don't say it, but they make me feel like they are talking to me and saying I am a n____." The other boys in the room nodded in agreement.

After a few moments, Chris addressed the continued silence, "Let's use the rest of the time to talk about what else you boys want to talk about." Billy immediately started up a conversation about how Obama (the U.S. president during the time of the study) was "aging a lot" and "turning gray because of all of the stress of the presidency." The boys all jumped on the topic, but soon the bell rang and I was saying goodbye to them.

The conversation that ensued that day in the Boys Group highlights how structural and interactional educational opportunity gaps, amplified by the diversifying social context of Sunderville, negatively impacted Black and Latinx males labeled with a disability. The tensions brewing from the shifting community context, coupled with educators' biases and preconceived notions about diverse students, alienated educators from students who were different from them. The tensions also fueled misunderstandings about students and reinforced negative stereotypes about Black and Latinx males, as evidenced in the stories of the boys in Chris's group.

In particular, in Simon's case, when he was sick in the stairwell he was not seen as a young man in need of help. Rather, he was treated as if he had already done something wrong and deserved punishment. The educators around him had already deemed him to be an offender and someone who did not deserve empathy, sympathy, or compassion. And, in his punishment, no one stopped to question whether or not their micro-actions and/or decisions further alienated him from the schooling process or limited his access to opportunities to learn. He was given the punishment prescribed for a student's failure to comply with school rules. No one stopped to think whether or not educators' beliefs and biases, or the social norms, systems, and structures of Sunderville School District contributed to an unfair punishment for a young man who wasn't feeling well.

Gerrytown: Divided Spaces and Educational Opportunity Gaps

Gerrytown was confronted with a different social contextual issue that affected how educators related to students and families in the district than Huntertown and Sunderville. Gerrytown wasn't demographically shifting; it is and has been a historically segregated and divided school district.

The town's business center is designed to look like a typical small-town main street. It is characterized by elements of visual cohesion, where storefronts look alike and several signs hang on the street's lampposts boasting Gerrytown's community pride. However, the idyllic façade of the business core is fleeting when you travel a short distance from Main Street.

A 5-minute drive in either direction presents two very different communities. Traveling east, the storefronts become less uniform, the road widens and becomes busier with speeding traffic, car shops, temporary housing structures, discount retailers, and fewer manicured lawns. Traveling west, however, the lawns maintain a distinct uniformity, stores and businesses boast products such as organic produce and teeth-whitening services, and the roads wind in various directions leading to cul-de-sacs nestled within semicircles of large houses.

Gerrytown School District is also racially and economically segregated. It operates under the Princeton Plan desegregation strategy, in which student attendance is organized by grade level, not by where students reside. Two of its four school buildings are within the most segregated areas, where predominantly Black and Latinx residents live; the other two border the predominantly white part of the community.

Initially, I was unaware of the racial and economic divisions within Gerrytown, but my naiveté did not last long. On my first day of fieldwork, I erroneously went to the central administration office rather than to the office where the director of special education, Roger Nero, was housed. I realized my error when speaking with the secretary in the central administration building.

I was anxious to meet Roger, and when I realized my mistake, I asked the secretary how I could walk to his office. She looked at me oddly and told me it was best if I did not walk because I would have to "cross a busy street" and it was "far." She told me she would call Roger and have him pick me up. While she dialed his number, I asked her how far away his office was from where we were. She told me that it was "less than a mile" away. I was surprised she didn't encourage me to walk, but went along with it.

Within 10 minutes of her calling Roger, I was in his car being driven several blocks toward the east side of town. While in the car, I realized that the secretary did not feel comfortable having me walk through the less "desirable" parts of the community as Roger labeled the area when we drove through it.

The educators in the district were aware that Gerrytown was divided. However, they tended to describe the segregation in the community and schools as a relatively normal fact of life. One grade school teacher noted that issues in Gerrytown surrounding "things like race and disproportionality" have "been going on for decades." A grade school psychologist told me "it is a divided community" and "there has always been a big difference between east Gerrytown and west Gerrytown." A high school psychologist told me there is a "real mix" of races and socioeconomic groups in Gerrytown. She added that the west side was a "million-dollar neighborhood," "beautiful," "very affluent," and "mostly white." She also told me that "pretty much all the white kids" attend private schools in Gerrytown. After some fact checking, I found that this was true and it also accounted for the low number of white students enrolled in the public school system. Another interviewee, a social worker, told me he thought Gerrytown was "very stable" with "legacies of families." When probed on what he meant by "legacy," he said, "it is a very segregated community with the whites in the west and Blacks in the east," implicating the lack of integration in the community. He was quick to add:

> There is racism here in this community. It's not overt but it is there.
> No one really talks about how segregated it is, but I mean, the
> district lives like we are separate but equal, just as long as equal
> means you don't join us! I think the community chooses to live like
> it is the 1950s because it is easier and making changes costs money.

Unfortunately, the more time I spent in the district, the more I realized that a majority of the district employees I interacted with did not connect how the segregated community and schools negatively affected educational practice. Instead, many of the professionals I spoke with and got to know confided in me during informal interviews and observations that they saw no issues with how children were treated, disciplined, or educated in Gerrytown. Rather, they used deficit-based language to describe students and attributed behavioral issues and academic failure to students' abilities or to their families' characteristics, and not to the lack of resources or educational opportunities in the public school system.

Essentially, the segregation was so normal and so historically embedded in the fabric of Gerrytown that people appeared to be rather unaffected by it. The educators seemed to downplay the salience of race and racial inequality in Gerrytown despite the fact that the majority of the student body was comprised of Black and Latinx students. This allowed for disproportionality to be rationalized and attributed to student characteristics rather than to educators' beliefs and biases, to the local context, or to broader opportunity gaps.

While in the field, I did find a small group of staff members who were outraged by the inequities they saw in the school system and by the segregation within the community, though. They were straightforward about their frustration and often shared it with me. An elementary school principal told me, "Gerrytown is a racist place," lamenting that students were treated as if "they were nothing." Others described feeling connected to the students within the public school community but they were saddened by how the district operated and treated its students. A high school guidance counselor was very clear about her frustration with the district: "It is an act of God that we [Gerrytown] have not been in the newspapers more. The way kids are treated here, it is like 'I'm done with you.' I'm surprised nothing worse has happened," referencing the district's citation for disproportionality. However, no matter how educators in Gerrytown related to the community context, there was a general sense of apathy among the staff about the teaching and learning conditions in Gerrytown changing. The divisions in the community were just too deep and the resulting educational opportunity gaps felt insurmountable.

DISPROPORTIONALITY IS COMPLEX

Educational opportunity gaps are deeply entrenched in the everyday educational practices of schools, and society more generally. They manifest when students are not provided with adequate opportunities to learn and are the product of both structural and interactional factors that collectively impact student outcomes. Educational opportunity gaps are also related to the educational debt owed to students of color (Ladson-Billings, 2006), which is a product of historical, economic, sociopolitical, and moral sources of inequity that have accumulated over time and negatively impact Black, Latinx, and Native American students in particular. Racially, culturally, and ethnically diverse students with disabilities are also subject to the impacts of the educational debt (Thorius & Tan, 2015), regardless of the promises of IDEA to provide *all* students with a free appropriate public education. This is because the legislative promise of IDEA cannot sufficiently counter the effects that local contextual social forces and educational opportunity gaps have on student outcomes.

In addition, when educators assume that adequate educational interventions and services have been given to students with disabilities, without serious consideration of the effects of local contextual factors on student outcomes, deficit-based beliefs about students are reinforced. A deficit-based lens does not interrogate how educational systems, educators' biases and beliefs, educational opportunity gaps, and/or resource inequalities relate to educational inequities. Linda Darling-Hammond (2013) explains how deficit thinking, linked to notions of equal educational opportunity, serves as a pernicious framework that ignores the multiple sources of inequality in the U.S. education system. She states:

> The assumption that equal educational opportunity now exists reinforces the belief that the causes of continued low levels of achievement on the part of students of color must be intrinsic to them, their families, or their communities. Educational outcomes of students of color are however, at least as much a function of their unequal access to key educational resources, both inside and outside of the school, as they are a function of race, class, or culture. (p. 79)

Thus, when opportunity gaps and social contextual factors are ignored, student failure is normalized. This allows for racial inequities to persist, because no one is held accountable for educational inequities, and compliance with a policy mandate(s) alone cannot sufficiently counter the complex historical and social forces that influence the unequal provision of educational opportunities across schools in the United States.

CHAPTER 3

The Crucial Role of Educational Leadership

Educational leaders—whether at the district or school level, special or general education—have a significant effect on the educational outcomes of the students they serve. School and district leaders not only manage how a district or school functions, but they also set priorities and the tone for how educational services are delivered within local contexts. According to Louis et al. (2010) and Leithwood, Seashore-Louis, Anderson, and Wahlstrom (2004), leadership's effect on student learning is second to teachers' and may even be underestimated. Similarly Bryk, Sebring, Allensworth, Luppescu, and Easton (2010), in their study on urban schools in Chicago, found that effective school-based leadership is one of the main "ingredients" needed to initiate school change processes, highlighting the critical role that educational leaders play in improving student outcomes. Bryk et al. (2010) also illustrate just how complex the work of an educational leader is as they find that school-based leaders must effectively manage and work with families and communities, develop and sustain a positive student climate and culture, nurture staff development, and ensure that there is curricular and instructional alignment in their schools in order to improve student outcomes. To put it simply, leadership matters, and leadership's impact extends across many aspects of the educational landscape.

LEADING FOR EQUITY

In schools and districts that are experiencing educational inequities like disproportionality, an educational leader's capacity to develop a strategic equity vision that addresses race and class inequities is critical for improving student outcomes. For instance, Skrla, Scheurich, Garcia, and Nolly (2004) found that in schools and districts that are facing inequities, it is essential for educational leaders to be engaged, willing to transform school culture, and focused on the success of all students as they work to address educational opportunity gaps. In addition, in Fergus's (2016) applied work on addressing disproportionality, he asserts that educational leaders must be purposeful in engaging their staff in conversations that directly address educators' biases and beliefs associated with race and class differences. Essentially, equity-focused leadership requires that leaders simultaneously make decisions about the allocation of educational resources, design and approve programs for practice, set the tone for how their staffs should educate students, challenge their staffs to unpack personal biases and beliefs, and positively influence school climate and staff morale while maintaining an unwavering focus on achieving educational equity for all students. This is not an easy task.

There are three reasons why it is difficult for district and school leaders to operate with a purposeful and coordinated plan that supports all students that relate to the findings in this study. First, educational leaders are engulfed in the social, political, and normative environments of their school districts, which have their own working understandings of what race, inequality, and special education mean to educators and community members. This can either limit or supplant their efforts to pursue educational equity and/or educational equality. Second, educational leaders filter their decisions through their own personal belief systems, which may include deficit-based views (Valencia & Solórzano, 1997) about students and families. These belief systems affect how educational leaders decide to allocate resources across school systems, and they also influence what school- and/or district-based initiatives leaders prioritize to improve student outcomes. Lastly, because the sources of disproportionality are complex and deeply embedded in the educational system (Harry & Klingner, 2014), educational leaders (along with other educational stakeholders) must systematically align educational policies, procedures, practices, and people in order to holistically address the issue (e.g., Klingner et al., 2005). The immense task associated with aligning educational policies, procedures, practices, and people can be overwhelming, but educational leaders cannot take the path of least resistance or make decisions that have not been thought through for their equity implications.

In addition, educational leaders must resist colorblind and race-neutral frameworks in their professional practice. If they rely upon these frameworks to administer educational policies, practices, and procedures, the mindset denies the significance of race in everyday life and it also justifies and naturalizes racialized outcomes like disproportionality. This is because it does not require that educators reflect on the role they play in the production of unequal outcomes. The framework also unintentionally reinforces deficit views about students, because their educational failure is attributed to individual capacities and not to contextual factors.

In Sunderville, Gerrytown, and Huntertown, which are and were experiencing racial inequities in special education, the leadership structures in each district did not systematically align resources to provide equal educational opportunity and access to all students. Rather, the leadership structures were highly influenced by local contextual factors and norms that maintained the status quo rather than challenge it. In addition, in all three districts, the leadership structures used standards-based, colorblind, and race-neutral frameworks to justify how educational services were delivered to students.

For instance, in Sunderville, the superintendent was focused on uniting his district and the school community amid the district's diversifying sociodemographic context. He promoted the use of standardized educational policies and practices in order to mute the tensions that arose from the community context, and this strategy contributed to the reproduction of racial inequities in disciplinary outcomes rather than addressing them. In Gerrytown, the superintendent and the central leadership team were very disconnected from the local schools and community context. People worked in silos, and there was no strategic or cohesive vision from the central leadership team that could unite the divided community and the lack of a unified equity vision coming from the superintendent within the highly segregated context negatively affected student outcomes. In Huntertown, the leadership structures were subject to the whim of parents. Whatever parents wanted in Huntertown, they got, and this negatively affected the students whose parents did not regularly demand resources and educational services from the district. In each case, the equity implications of the educational leaders' actions were never examined, and this impacted how disproportionality was understood and addressed, because without a strategic and comprehensive vision to address disproportionality that went beyond compliance with IDEA, the issue could not and would not be resolved.

Sunderville: Systemic Issues, Simple Solutions

Dr. Lovene was the superintendent of Sunderville School District, and he was both loved and feared. He was charismatic and appealed to the hearts and minds of the community members and staff in the district. He was also very public facing and was known for invoking the notion of "Sunderville Pride," using personal stories about his experiences in Sunderville to foster a sense of community and belonging in the school district. In board meetings, newsletters, district announcements on the website, and other such public forums, Dr. Lovene would call up "Sunderville Pride," saying, "We are a proud community" and "We are Sunderville strong." He was focused on making sure that the people within the school district had a cohesive identity, and most staff within the district appreciated his efforts.

For instance, educators in Sunderville rarely spoke negatively of, or about, Dr. Lovene. In informal interviews and conversations with multiple staff members, I would hear expressions of adulation and praise for him. When I asked a district employee to share his thoughts on Dr. Lovene, he eagerly replied:

Dr. Lovene is so great. He is awesome! I love him! There is no other man in his category!! He is like a great leader on steroids. He attended Sunderville and was an administrator here. He is a real stand-up guy!!!

The same employee told me that Dr. Lovene "wanted to retire for the past 2 school years but decided to stay on as superintendent because he wants to stay with us and help us through the rough waters," referring to the tensions stemming from the demographic shifts. He later added, "I am in awe of him." This employee was emotional when he spoke about Dr. Lovene, and he felt a very strong connection with him. Dr. Lovene had almost a mythic status among his employees.

When I would probe staff to discuss whether or not Dr. Lovene's leadership style effectively addressed inequities in Sunderville, they would shy away from criticizing him, his leadership style, and/or his policy and practice recommendations. He was a seemingly untouchable figure, and his directives were followed without much debate or criticism. However, the tight rein that Dr. Lovene had on his staff unintentionally adversely affected the district's ability to address a systemic inequity like disproportionality.

In particular, early on in the year of research, the Sunderville Board of Education toured the high school and saw that there were many students walking the halls and not in class. According to Marc, the board members were very upset by what they saw and complained to Dr. Lovene that something had to be done to stop the "truancy issue." Dr. Lovene swiftly enacted a districtwide policy called "hall sweeps," which was carried out primarily in the middle and high schools.

The disciplinary practice consisted of adults patrolling school halls and rounding up students whom they found walking around after the bell had rung for class. Students caught in a sweep were brought to the school's auditorium, where they had to sit until administration could reach their parents or guardians. The expectation was that the parent or guardian would have to immediately pick the student up from school and take him or her home. If a parent or guardian could not immediately get the child, the student would be suspended from school.

Hall sweeps drastically increased the number of suspensions in the district and persisted for many months. The practice was enacted despite consecutive years of disproportionality citations for inequitable disciplinary practices in Sunderville. And the practice was enacted despite the fact that many of the students "caught" in the sweeps were those who were already affected by disproportionality in the district; they included students with disabilities, Black and Latinx students, and/or less affluent White students.

The hall sweeps were publicly celebrated for months. They were highlighted on the district website and in newsletters sent home to parents and/or guardians. The messages referring to the hall sweeps invoked "Sunderville Pride" and they directly urged students and parents to "rise up" to the "high expectations" of the district. The announcements, whether online or in person, rationalized the suspensions of hundreds of students gathered up in hall sweeps. And Dr. Lovene signed off on these messages and unflinchingly defended the practice in board meetings.

I often heard staff openly support the practice in both public and private forums. I even heard some staff call them "fun" to administer. I clearly observed how this mentality manifested in practice when I attended a special education meeting in the high school. Right before the meeting was going to start, one of the high school assistant principals entered the room, sat down loudly, and slammed a clipboard on the table that had a pile of "write-ups" attached. The write-ups were blank disciplinary referrals used to justify a suspension from a hall sweep. The teacher sitting next to me looked at the administrator and asked, "How many have you written up today?" It was only an hour into the school day. The administrator answered laughing, "None yet, but I'm ready!" She appeared to be very enthusiastic about the prospect of using the write-ups. No one reacted and the meeting began shortly thereafter.

Marc knew the assistant principal who attended this meeting well and he told me that he thought that the sweeps "worked" to "clean up the halls," but he also thought that educators like this assistant principal relied on the hall sweeps too much as a disciplinary intervention. He said there are "APs [assistant principals] there at the high school who just sit in their office [saying], 'Next,' you know, 'out of school,' 'next,' 'in school,' 'next,' and that's it all day long. That's all that happens." He was describing the high school administration's tendency to uncritically hand out either an "in-school" or "out-of-school" suspension without realizing the consequences of their actions on students' lives.

Through hall sweeps Dr. Lovene essentially promoted the idea that his staff use a colorblind and zero-tolerance approach to discipline. While he had good intentions designed to achieve safe and orderly schools, the way in which he approached the issue and instructed his staff to address truancy had racialized outcomes. The policy approach also exacerbated stereotypes and biases about diverse students that were already present in the district.

For instance, I found a few staff members who would express to me in private that they felt some trepidation about complying with and enacting the disciplinary policy and practice. However, regardless of this feeling, they still took part in administering hall sweeps. A building leader described to me his experiences observing his staff using the policy and how hall sweeps intersected with disproportionality and race. He told me a story about a Black middle-schooler named Jonathon:

> Sometimes I think about how, sometimes, you see this kid walking out [in the halls]. You have this kid, you have Jonathon. . . . I hate to say it, but he's always in the hall. He's always the last kid

in the hall and he causes problems here. People see him walking down the hall. . . . Teachers see him and you see a 6'3" Black kid walking down the hall. You don't see a 14-year-old walking down the hall. You see a 6'3" Black kid, and that scares some people, and people are offended by him and he gets suspended.

Hall sweeps strengthened existing negative perceptions and stereotypes about students, in particular Black and Latinx students, and the administrator seemed to be worried about this. He thought the educational practice allowed his staff to see an "offender" walking the halls rather than a child: a 14-year-old boy who might need redirection or help in school. Despite the administrator's awareness about this, though, he was clear in his interview that he "liked policies like hall sweeps," because the halls were less chaotic after the bell rang.

One day, after attending a special education meeting with a teacher who often sought me out to discuss disproportionality, I got an honest look into how she felt about hall sweeps and Dr. Lovene's tight rein. She told me:

I don't understand how this [hall sweeps] even makes sense because kids are getting what they want, which is to be out of school, and they are not being helped. The school doesn't offer enough alternative services for kids to get the help they need. . . . I get it why they are doing it to clean up the halls, but at the same time I don't really get it. What will they [students] learn? To just keep getting suspended? Administration's vision is very linear, but they have to be because they don't have time to spend on this stuff [alternatives to suspension] because there is so much other stuff, like testing and compliance.

Essentially, she expressed what I could clearly see, which was that the students who were most affected by hall sweeps were the ones who needed something else, a different kind of educational intervention, to succeed in the district. However, the district's norms and priorities did not align with this need and staff followed Dr. Lovene's vision at any cost.

It was not until late in the school year when the practice adversely affected more high-achieving students with influential parents that Dr. Lovene asked that the practice be amended. This occurred after a contentious board meeting where a high-achieving white student's parent publicly fought the board and Dr. Lovene about the rationale behind hall sweeps. The parent demanded that the superintendent and the board justify why his child was suspended for being "2 minutes late to class." As one result of this board meeting, hall sweeps were phased out by the end of the school year. However, regardless of the change in course, the damage was already done to the students who had been affected by hall sweeps; they had multiple suspensions and missed many days of school.

In summary, even though Dr. Lovene was a strong leader with a vision, the way in which he mobilized educational resources, policies, practices, procedures, and people exacerbated inequities rather than addressing them. And the policy of hall sweeps undermined the very notion of "Sunderville Pride" that Dr. Lovene was using to bring people together. Instead of uniting students, staff, and community members to "rise up" to the high expectations of the district, hall sweeps further alienated staff from students and contributed to the high number of suspensions in the district. The use of hall sweeps also meant that Sunderville would once again be cited for disproportionality in disciplinary outcomes in the 2012–2013 school year for both white and Black students.

Gerrytown: Detached Leadership

Unlike Sunderville, the educators in Gerrytown did not have a strong leader or comprehensive educational mission and vision that they could follow when serving students and families in the district. In addition, the disconnect between the public school community and the leadership structures in Gerrytown negatively affected staff morale and impacted how students and families were served. This was extremely consequential in a place like Gerrytown, because the district's history of inequities, coupled with the community and district's segregation, required strong leadership structures that could unite the fragmented school system.

I spoke with several building leaders who told me that they didn't pay much attention to the superintendent's and central leadership team's mandates. An elementary school building principal told me she didn't feel like the superintendent and his colleagues respected her work, the families in the district, or the students in her school. These sentiments manifested in practice when the high needs of the community intersected with school district structures.

For instance, one day I attended the kindergarten registration process held in one-half of the elementary school gym. Almost immediately after 8 a.m., a line formed in the school halls and the gym became cramped, full of people, noise, and humid air. A large partition had been erected in the middle of the gym and on the other half of the gym was a group of kindergartners having gym class. Every so often, I would hear children's laughter and the occasional blaring of a popular cartoon theme song crackling from speakers on the other side of the gym. The half of the gym that I was in had eight folding tables set up in an L-shaped pattern that was meant to physically direct parents through the registration process. Two secretaries were behind one table with a copy machine; at another table sat the school nurse; and behind the rest of the tables were school personnel sorting papers. Each person was highly preoccupied with determining whether or not parents had brought in the proper forms for registration.

Several hours passed with a dull din constantly filling the gym, defined by the whir of copy machines, secretaries yelling "next," parents talking, and pens scraping on forms. During the 3 hours I stayed in the gym, not one staff member was able to sit down. Everyone seemed stressed, both staff and parents, because there was a tangible feeling that there weren't enough staff members, translators, or support people present to help move the registration process along.

At one point, the elementary school principal came into the gym and she spoke with me about how disappointed she felt when watching the registration process. She said that she was frustrated that her building was the only one in the district that had specifically hired a Spanish-speaking staff member to communicate with parents. She also added that she didn't understand why the superintendent didn't mandate that all schools hire at least one bilingual staff member because of the linguistic and cultural diversity of the district's students and families.

Dr. Gerald, the district superintendent, also stopped by the gym midway through the registration process with a photographer from the local newspaper. He was taking part in a news story that was being written about private school students who initiated a food collection project for homeless students registered in the public school system. Dr. Gerald briefly peeked into the gym, waved, and walked away with the reporter. During this time, I noticed staff members looking very frustrated and angry at the sight of him. One secretary told me that when he left, she felt relieved.

The themes raised in this ethnographic moment surfaced and resurfaced throughout my fieldwork. There were never enough resources to accommodate the diverse needs of the families and students in Gerrytown. And Dr. Gerald, and his leadership team more broadly, were not pro-active or reactive to these needs. Rather, they seemed distant and far removed from the concerns and needs of both educators and families in the school district. This occurred despite the fact that Dr. Gerald and his team had built in and created many administrative positions in hopes that the needs of students and families could be better met.

Roger told me that Gerrytown School District was "top heavy," in reference to the numerous directors and school-based leaders in the district, but he also told me that the plethora of leaders rarely worked together cohesively to achieve an outcome. Often, district-based initiatives would stop and start in fits in the district's schools and the schools tended to operate as independent silos. This was because the initiatives that did come from central administration were not tailored to students' needs, and they often felt "disconnected" from the social realities of the student body, as Roger told me.

There was one school building in the district, a middle school, that did take up the central administration's initiatives with full force. The principal and assistant principal of this building had close ties to the superintendent's office. However, despite these connections, the central administration's initiatives rarely lasted long and/or rarely made a significant positive difference on student outcomes in the middle school.

Roger once shared a story with me about how state auditors came to the district to perform a comprehensive review of this middle school, the one that had close ties to the central leadership team, because it had consistently poor academic outcomes. Roger said that the state auditors came up with "two big findings." The first was that "there is no curriculum" and the second is that "there is no lesson-planning structure." Roger was frustrated because the review had been conducted months prior to my discussion with him and "the [building-level] administration [had] not done anything about the findings to date." He added that the state auditors also conducted focus groups with some students in the middle school and "they [the students] all expressed to the state they do not feel safe, but nobody did a thing about it." Yet the central administrative team often heralded this middle school as a model school and encouraged staff to pay attention to the best practices occurring in the building during professional development sessions.

While in the field, I also observed and heard of evidence that the central administrative team actively pushed staff to deny educational resources to vulnerable students in order to control costs. For example, the district had a growing population of homeless students that was not well served. This group of students was a persistent concern for the educators within the school buildings. Despite this fact, the superintendent's team encouraged staff not to inform parents of their educational rights under federal homeless law because "it would cost too much to service them [the homeless students]," as one high-level leader said in a cabinet meeting I attended. An elementary school social worker told me a story about a homeless child she wanted to help, but didn't, because an individual from the central leadership team encouraged her not to tell the student's family about the services they were legally entitled to under the McKinney-Vento Homeless Assistance Act. When I asked why the high-level district official said this to her, she shared that it was because the funds that would be used "to help that one child" needed to be aligned toward "other matters" in the district. There were numerous times throughout my fieldwork where I observed dynamics like this—an indifference to the needs of students from high-level leaders—play out and negatively affect students and the climate and culture of the district.

For instance, in a monthly directors meeting that I attended in the late fall, which was supposed to address a bullying incident that had occurred in the middle school, I observed how a serious topic like bullying received symbolic and superficial treatment from the superintendent. The directors meeting was led by the superintendent, Dr. Gerald, and all of the district's directors, administrators, and central administration staff were in attendance.

Once all of the directors had settled into their chairs, Dr. Gerald handed out a five-page stapled document entitled "Harassment and Bullying Policy." He stated, "I am handing this out because the more bullying policy gets media attention, the more parents are going to ask for it." As the papers were passed around he added, "I am giving you the packet because a parent recently asked for it and a teacher couldn't find it." The room was quiet, yet loud with the noise of papers moving in an assembly line through the hands of the approximately 30 directors in the room. I distinctly remember feeling awkward as I ceremoniously flipped through the pages of the packet, copying the actions of others in the room.

After about 3 minutes of paper shuffling, Dr. Gerald sat back in his chair and asked, "Does anyone have any questions?" Dr. Gerald did not ask the leadership team to examine issues of bullying in the district or discuss the bullying policy's message. He also did not contextualize the conversation within some of the major bullying incidents that had occurred in one of the middle schools in the district.

After some time, a grade school principal raised his hand and asked, "Just curious, because a teacher recently asked me, do we have a [districtwide] policy manual?" The room rippled with uncomfortable laughter, and a woman sitting next to me said loudly, "Yeah, it's from like 1990!" The manual the principal was asking about had the district's vision and mission statement written in it, but very few of the educators in the room knew it existed. The majority of the directors and administrators in the room also indicated that they were unaware that a districtwide policy manual should be shared with parents and guardians in the beginning of the school year. Dr. Gerald did not appear to be concerned or alarmed by this. He also did not discuss the district's mission and vision statement with his staff. Instead, Dr. Gerald sat back in his chair and watched his staff talk.

After a few minutes of back-and-forth among the staff about the district-wide policy manual, Dr. Gerald addressed the chatter by stating, "The policy manual is outdated," but that it was "periodically updated for compliance reasons." He also added that the manual was "in the process of being entirely" updated but it was not ready yet. He said that when it was finished, he would let them know. He then asked if there were any more questions about the bullying policy. The room was silent, and Dr. Gerald moved on to the next agenda item. Bullying was not discussed again in the meeting.

Roger was deeply affected by the tone that the central leadership team set for the staff across the district. He told me that "the lack of urgency" to help students in Gerrytown "baffled" him. An elementary school principal, who was an ally of Roger's, lamented that "leadership [at the building level] has no power here," and that "the superintendent is not effective, and he will not come down with a hammer" to force educators to "do the right thing for kids." Other staff members I spoke with who were close to Roger expressed anger about the "flippancy" and "disregard" central leadership exhibited toward students, as a middle school teacher described to me. Unfortunately, these feelings left many staff members feeling exhausted and apathetic about the poor academic and behavioral outcomes of students, because they felt powerless to change the teaching and learning conditions in Gerrytown. And in a community like Gerrytown, where the historical legacy of segregation and failed integration greatly influenced the schooling process, if leadership didn't have a cohesive and strategic vision for equity that could motivate educators in the district, then systemic inequities were likely to persist.

Huntertown: Who Is Actually Leading?

The equity issues that emerged from the intersections between the local community context and leadership structures in Huntertown were very different from those in Sunderville and Gerrytown. The district was not rapidly diversifying like Sunderville and it was not characterized by a deeply segregated school system like Gerrytown. Rather, Huntertown is a cohesive and stable community, and there were very strong social norms at play that affected how leaders could lead and how educators could educate students. However, although Huntertown presented a very different community context than the other two districts, the district's equity issues were also related to weak leadership structures, but the reasons behind why the leadership structures were ineffective in achieving equity varied.

Social Cohesion and the Huntertown Family. The community of Huntertown has been relatively racially stable for decades, with very little fluctuation in the community's sociodemographic composition. It is a primarily white, wealthy, and demographically stable community and school district. The lack of sociodemographic changes in Huntertown was noticed at the federal level in the late 1990s, when the Department of Justice conducted an inquiry into possible racial housing discrimination. Although the report concluded that Huntertown did not have any evidence of "active discrimination," the report did raise concerns about the community's persistent racial homogeneity.

While in the field, I found that many of the educators I met took pride in the cultural cohesiveness and stability of the community and it influenced how they understood and related to students and families. When I would interview various staff members and ask them questions about the community context, I realized that they struggled to define things like "diversity" and speak about diversity in the context of Huntertown. For instance, in an interview with an elementary school teacher, I had to spend about 5 minutes unpacking what the term *diversity* meant when I asked her if she thought Huntertown was diverse. She struggled to identify points of racial, class, and/or linguistic diversity in her school. She did tell me though, that there are a lot of Italian and Irish families in the district, but that Huntertown is "relatively stable in terms of its diversity." She also added that "diversity" was not a defining characteristic of Huntertown. What I often found was that the educators in the district could speak about the "typical" Huntertown student, but they struggled to speak about students who existed outside the Huntertown "norm." This affected how students experienced schooling in Huntertown, too.

For instance, in a conversation with the superintendent of curriculum and instruction, he told me that he found it "fascinating" when recent graduates returned to visit with him and reflect on their experiences in Huntertown. He told me that the students "often express they felt pigeonholed" into an identity that "they had trouble escaping while in the district." He also added that students often said that they "did not feel exposed enough" to "diversity" while attending school in Huntertown. He said that some students he recently spoke with told him they were "surprised" and "shocked" by the "diversity of the world." In a similar vein, a social worker recounted her initial thoughts when she began working in the district. She said, "I called my friend and told her I feel like I just went back into 1955" adding, "cheerleaders and football players are rewarded here," and "if you aren't a musician or an actor or something, you [as a student] will have a hard time." She told me that she "feared for" the students who were "a little different," because Huntertown was not open to these differences.

I found that the newest employees in the district, those who had started working in the district within the past 5 years, were able to describe the diversity in Huntertown more clearly. They tended to be more open about what the lack of diversity meant for the community, school district, and students. For example, a school building leader who was new to the district in the year of research said in an interview,

> It's [Huntertown] a very tight-knit community with people here that have history and family. And that all makes a really wonderful, you know, such a wonderful community. . . . But is it diverse? Not really, no, no. And I don't know if they [the people of Huntertown] yet embrace diversity. I don't think that they don't embrace it, but I'm not sure if they embrace diversity or if they welcome it. I don't mean that necessarily that it's a racist community . . . but the roots are very, very deep here.

Even though Huntertown was not a "racist community," the administrator seemed to struggle with her knowledge that people in the district did not embrace differences or change. And, after some time in the field, I found out that the "roots" the administrator spoke about translated into a phrase, the "Huntertown family," that I often heard while in the district. The phrase was used by district families and staff to promote "a sense of wholeness and belonging in the school," as one teacher told me. The phrase also served as a symbolic boundary that signaled who belonged in the community and who didn't. It often had racial tones, too.

For instance, of the 25 formal and informal interviews I conducted in Huntertown, only three interviewees critiqued the strong norms associated with the notion of the Huntertown family. A secretary told me that she "loved" Huntertown and the "Huntertown family" as she "attended school in the district," and "now works for the district," but that she also struggles with how staff members treat some students. She told me she knew the community was "not very tolerant" of differences and that parents could be very "demanding." She added that certain students, mostly students of color or students with disabilities, could be "treated poorly," and that some of her colleagues spoke to students who were "a little different . . . like [they were] monkeys." Another staff member in this group of interviewees shared an experience that left her feeling "limited" in what she could teach her students. She told me that the day after she taught her 10th-grade class a poem written by a Black female author, she received several visits and phone calls from parents who felt "uncomfortable" with the content of her lesson. She said that the parents asked her not to use teaching material "like that kind" again. She felt she could not freely make curricular decisions because she feared strong parent backlash or pushback from her colleagues. Ironically, though, shortly after sharing her story with me, she said that "I love" working in Huntertown because the staff was "so great to me in my times of need." The norms associated with being part of the "Huntertown family" were strong and also affected how leaders could lead.

Limited Leadership. The leadership structure in Huntertown was at the whim of the community's norms and ways of being. From the superintendent's office down, leadership, whether at the district or school building level, almost always did what the parents and community members wanted them to do. Some leaders were OK with this, while others were uncomfortable with the amount of power and persuasion the community had on the school system.

For example, the high school principal was proud of his relationship with parents. He described the district as a "private school system" because of how much power parents have over district operations. Others, who were relatively new to the district and/or had not grown up in or did not have family ties to Huntertown, were more vocal about the negative repercussions of high parent involvement on their capacity to lead. An elementary school building leader, who had been working in the district for 8 years, candidly expressed her disdain over how much the district catered to parent demands:

> I feel like the district is co-opting with parents. . . . I record everything
> I do so I can't be held liable for anything that might go wrong or
> that a parent doesn't like. . . . I feel bullied and I start to sweat
> just thinking about them [the parents]. Sometimes at the board
> meetings I just feel sick. . . . I really struggle with how much the
> parents stress me out. How can I protect the kids, my staff, and
> my own job when parents are so combative? For example, once a
> parent said something about one of my teachers and now no one
> wants to be in that teacher's class but the teacher is actually really
> good. I mean, after one particularly bad board meeting, a parent,
> [one] that isn't combative, brought me a muffin in the morning
> because she felt so bad for me! What if I lose my [administrative]
> certification because of the parents that are so intense?

While her worries seemed extreme, they were well grounded. I witnessed several board meetings where parents acted as direct consumers of educational services and completely influenced the professional decisions of the educators and administrators in the district.

For instance, in a board meeting held in the beginning of the school year, the assistant superintendent gave a presentation about a math program that the district offices wanted to adopt. He presented a comprehensive rationale for the program and offered data to support the effectiveness of the program. However, a group of particularly vocal parents openly contested the proposed math program in the board meeting. Over the next few weeks, several parents banded together to formally oppose the program and it was not adopted by the district, regardless of the expertise of the educational professional recommending the service.

I also observed how a group of parents in Huntertown was able to oust a high-level district leader from her position. A group of district parents drafted an anonymous letter and distributed it to every resident in Huntertown who had a child or children enrolled in the district in the late fall. Cynthia, who had gotten hold of the letter, told me the letter contained personal and professional slander against the high-level official. Cynthia had her own issues with the leader, but she did not think that the things written in the letter accurately represented the official's professional capacities.

During a school board meeting that was held about 5 months into the new school year, the high-level district leader announced her resignation. I was sitting in the crowd and heard chatter around me concerning the administrator's seemingly abrupt resignation. One woman next to me said, "That letter was full of really nasty things," and it was "a total smear" aimed to "banish" the district leader. I also heard a parent nearby say, "Well, the letter worked!" I heard only one parent say that she was saddened by the "smear campaign" and she did not agree with how the issue had been handled. Essentially, public school parents were able to exert enough pressure on school district officials to influence a high-level leader to resign because they were not happy with her services.

Once, during a personal one-on-one conversation I was having with Cynthia in her office about parents and the tone of board meetings, I asked her if she had ever let the parents and/or community members know that the district had a history of disproportionality citations. When I asked her this, she looked at me incredulously and said, "Could you imagine how they [the parents] would murder me if I told them about disproportionality!??" I asked her what she meant by that and what she thought would happen if she did publicly share knowledge of the citation. She answered,

> Board meetings are a sea of white faces and you just can't explain disproportionality to them. ELA (English language arts) scores are more important to these people than is disproportionality and we have people, staff, administrators that in this climate have to protect their jobs. They are facing foreclosures, bills, and other economic hardships and their jobs cannot be in jeopardy. It's not right to talk about this stuff in the meeting.

After seeing what had happened with the anonymous letter, I knew Cynthia had a point, but I felt as though Cynthia, along with a considerable number of her colleagues, was afraid to disrupt the social context, the taken-for-granted culture, and the social cohesion of Huntertown. She, along with most of the educators I met in Huntertown, appeared to shy away from challenging the local norms and ways of being that operated in Huntertown. And because of this, district and school building leaders did not make it a priority to realign resources to equitably serve all students in the district because they didn't need to; community members didn't demand it and therefore they didn't feel pressure to do so. Rather, it was much easier and more comfortable for the educators in Huntertown not to acknowledge racial inequities and to continue to essentially deny the salience of race in a district that has a historical legacy of racial inequities in special education.

ENACTING CHANGE FOR EDUCATIONAL EQUITY

The work of an educational leader, from the district to the school building level, is incredibly complex, but also crucially important in setting the tone for how students will be served in schools. Leaders have to manage multiple resource, professional, and normative pressures and constraints, which influences how they can direct their staff to serve the students before them. And, in school systems where an inequity like disproportionality is present, their influence is even more important, because they have the power to challenge and realign how educational policies, procedures, and practices are used to achieve a specific outcome.

Engaging in equity-focused leadership requires that educational leaders resist using simple solutions to address complex equity problems that are enshrouded in colorblind and race-neutral frameworks. Leaders must also be visionary and inclusive, and think systematically about the impacts of their decisions on student outcomes. They must be attuned to the negative assumptions and biases that they and their staff might have about students regarding their race, class, and intelligence. They must be ready to address these biases with their staff in the pursuit of educational equity because if these beliefs are ignored and/or normalized, then historically marginalized students will continue to be negatively affected and inequities will persist. Essentially, educational leaders have to be cultural change agents (Cooper, 2009). They cannot simply comply with the status quo, because the status quo means that educational inequities will be (and are) reproduced on a daily basis. Unfortunately, this visionary, inclusive leadership approach was not evident in the three districts included in this study.

The rigid disciplinary policies that were used in Sunderville, promoted and supported by the superintendent, negatively affected the culture and climate of the school district. Although educators enacted the race-neutral policy of hall sweeps with good intentions, their usage inadvertently reinforced negative stereotypes about Black and Latinx students and perpetuated disciplinary inequities. In Gerrytown, the fragmented and disjointed leadership structures, from the central administration offices down to the school buildings, allowed educators to use policies in superficial and symbolic ways that negatively affected student outcomes and staff morale. And, in Huntertown, educators and leaders were submissive to parents and to the norms of the local community context. These norms were based on a white normative framework that was not very tolerant of diversity. Collectively, in all three districts, the various leadership structures were complicit with local deficit-based beliefs about a student's race, class, and intelligence. The educators and leaders in Sunderville, Gerrytown, and Huntertown did not develop and work with equity visions that challenged social norms, ways of being, and/or biases associated with race and class differences, and this ultimately limited educational opportunities for diverse students, particularly Black and Latinx students, in each district.

CHAPTER 4

Parental "Power" and IDEA

Parental education, socioeconomic status, and family resources cast a "long shadow" (Alexander, Entwisle, & Olson, 2014) on children's educational attainment and social mobility. Decades of sociological research, primarily quantitative, have shown that a parent's occupational status largely determines their child's occupational status in a socially stratified system (Alexander et al., 2014; Blau & Duncan, 1967; Hout, 1988; Sewell, Haller, & Portes, 1969; Sewell & Shah, 1967). Psychosocial (Hauser, Tsai, & Sewell, 1983), school quality (Lucas, 2001), gender (Buchman & DiPrete, 2006; Mare & Maralani, 2006), and life course transition (Warren, Sheridan, & Hauser, 2002) factors have been identified as contributing factors to these patterns of stratification. Stratification research also indicates that educational attainment has some mediating effects on the seemingly durable relationship between family resources and a child's educational attainment and social mobility (Hout & DiPrete, 2006).

Many qualitative studies have also explored the relationship between parental resources and children's educational attainment (e.g., Lareau, 2002; Lewis-McCoy, 2014; MacLeod, 2008). These studies often invoke Pierre Bourdieu's (1977) theory on cultural and social capital, which has been utilized to understand how schools reward certain types of behaviors and ways of being, which in turn sustains and reproduces broader class-based inequalities. This perspective is useful for understanding how parental resources, IDEA mandates, and disproportionality are interrelated.

SOCIAL REPRODUCTION AND EDUCATIONAL OUTCOMES

According to Bourdieu (1977), individuals are socialized in their families and communities and develop class-specific ways of being, or "habitus." Habitus is a theoretical concept that describes a person's dispositions, tastes, preferences, and habits, and it determines "one's view of the world and one's place in it" (Dumais, 2002). Habitus serves as a form of cultural capital that can be used as currency to gain social advantages. Cultural capital can include such things as linguistic and cultural competencies, notions of entitlement, interactional styles, and so forth. Both habitus and cultural capital serve as mechanisms that reproduce systems of inequality, because cultural capital is both convertible and transmissible across generations (Bourdieu & Passeron, 1977). In other words, individuals can use their cultural capital to gain economic and/or social advantages, which then enables them to extend and reinforce their power and privilege across multiple social domains, and these social privileges are transmitted to their children.

Schools serve as a primary site for rewarding specific habitus and cultural capital because schools validate the "instruments of appropriation" (Bourdieu, 1977, p. 79), or habitus of the dominant culture. MacLeod (2008) summarizes how this process occurs by outlining four points associated with Bourdieu's work on social reproduction, cultural capital, and schools:

> First, distinctive cultural capital is transmitted by each social class. Second, the school systematically valorizes upper-class cultural capital and depreciates the cultural capital of the lower classes. Third, differential academic achievement is retranslated back into economic wealth—the job market remunerates the superior academic credentials earned mainly by the upper classes. Finally, the school legitimizes this process "by making social hierarchies and the reproduction of those hierarchies appear to be based upon the hierarchy of 'gifts,' merits, or skills established and ratified by its sanctions, or, in a word, by converting social hierarchies into academic hierarchies." (Bourdieu, 1977, cited in MacLeod, 2008, p. 14)

Schools essentially reward class-specific ways of being that systematically disadvantage some people over others. The process is seemingly invisible because it is so unquestioningly engrained in the way schools and society operate.

Annette Lareau, in her book *Unequal Childhoods* (2011), used Bourdieu's framework to analyze how inequality is related to parental interactions with educational professionals and the institution of schooling. She found that parents of lower socioeconomic status tended to trust in schools and not demand much from educators, which disadvantaged their children. On the other hand, higher socioeconomic families were able to customize their children's education and negotiate with professionals to benefit their children. Lareau's work, and Bourdieu more generally, have been incredibly influential and insightful for understanding the social mechanisms that allow for class-based inequality to reproduce in schools, but their focus on class arrangements inadvertently minimizes the significance of race on patterns of educational inequality.

Lewis-McCoy (2014), in his study on educational inequality in a wealthy suburban school district, expanded upon Lareau's work by situating it in relationship with Ogbu (1979, 1987) and Fordham and Ogbu's (1986) work on race and oppositional culture. Lewis-McCoy (2014) argues that neither a class-based description of inequality like Lareau's, nor a "deficit model of race" (p. 8) like Ogbu's, sufficiently accounts for how inequality is reproduced in schools. Rather, Lewis-McCoy (2014) argues that class-based material realities must be linked to racial ideologies in order to explain how inequality occurs and reoccurs in suburban schools. Essentially, Lewis-McCoy's (2014) work shows how inequality is not only associated with class-based social and cultural capital like Lareau's analysis implies; it is also associated with local dynamics of social power and privilege that are influenced by dominant racial ideologies, like colorblindness, that are operating within school systems, thus providing an intersectional analysis between race, class, and inequality.

Specifically, Lewis-McCoy (2014) used the concept of "opportunity hoarding" (Tilly, 1998) to describe the "missing link" between class and race-based explanations of inequality. Tilly (1998) defines opportunity hoarding as a process whereby "members of a categorically bounded network acquire access to a resource that is valuable, renewable, subject to monopoly, supportive of network activities, and enhanced by the network's modus operandi," which thus allows "network members [to] regularly hoard their access to the resource, creating beliefs and practices that sustain their control" (p. 91). Essentially, opportunity hoarding is a social practice that produces inequality and racial inequities. However, these inequities are justified and rationalized through a set of belief systems that are linked to racial ideologies like colorblindness. This is because such racial ideologies "are always grounded in material realities, embedded in institutions and [in] concrete social practices." This exposes a critical link between material objects and ideological systems that produces "real social outcomes" (Burke, 2017, p. 862). Essentially, colorblindness is not just a belief system that drives actions, but it is also a belief system that organizes resources, which ultimately generates racial inequalities (e.g., Bonilla-Silva, 2015). Therefore, when the notion of opportunity hoarding is applied to schools, as in Lewis-McCoy's work, it exposes how parental social power and economic privileges can be used to produce racial outcomes, which are then justified and rationalized away through a colorblind lens.

Opportunity hoarding is incredibly relevant to IDEA and disproportionality because it links the material resources that parents can garner through IDEA mandates to patterns of racial inequality. Because, as Wakelin (2008) notes, a parent's capacity to use the legislation to benefit his or her child is highly dependent upon one's wealth, knowledge of the student's rights through IDEA, and educational level. Research has also shown that wealthier, and often white, parents have historically been able to leverage IDEA to benefit their children the most (Ong-Dean, 2009; Pollock, 2010). In addition, Blanchett (2010), in her discussion of how race, class, and culture relate to the provision of educational services through IDEA, argues that white families often seek eligibility for "privileged" disability categories that have more positive connotations and allow for access to better educational services; however, they do so without being explicitly racist and without intending to produce racialized outcomes (a colorblind approach). These findings illustrate how the power granted to parents through IDEA may actually encourage social practices like opportunity hoarding, which, in turn, exacerbate racial inequities.

SPECIAL EDUCATION AND OPPORTUNITY HOARDING

Parents have always been central to the development of disability legislation. However, since the passage of IDEA in 1990, and with its subsequent reauthorization in 2004, parents have been given a considerable amount of power through "parental consent" to influence how their child is educated within LEAs. Parental consent has evolved to become one of the primary enforcement mechanisms behind IDEA because the federal government has rarely withheld IDEA funds when an SEA or an LEA does not comply with IDEA and local enforcement of IDEA by SEAs is inconsistent at best, especially in relationship to disproportionality (e.g., Albrecht et al., 2012; Cavendish, Artiles, & Harry 2014; Hehir, 2002; Wrightslaw, n.d.). This has equity implications because the policy mechanisms that parents can leverage for their child through IDEA are fraught with unintended consequences that contribute to race and class inequalities.

For example, the legal mechanisms that give parents the right to due process through IDEA are written in complicated language, require mastery of English, and are difficult to leverage without legal counsel. And, although due process is a strong mechanism for enforcement, many parents do not know their rights or know that they can challenge the decisions made by an IEP team (Hyman, Rivkin, & Rosenbaum, 2011). In addition, through IDEA, parents must give informed consent for any evaluations, labels, and/ or services suggested by a school or school district. Parents can also dispute a school's recommendation on how their child will be educated. However, Ong-Dean (2009), in his study on parental advocacy and IDEA, notes that "despite the legal mandate for parents' involvement in special education, decision making is often dominated by school administrators, special education teachers, and school psychologists, who cast themselves as having essential scientific (and legal) knowledge that parents lack" (p. 45). But, if parents and/or guardians have material wealth and/or connections to important social resources such as school boards, educational professionals, and/or legal advocates, they can use special education legislation to hoard opportunities for their children and override the professional opinions of educators.

The process of opportunity hoarding produces racial outcomes because it is often enacted within a colorblind framework that does not acknowledge the social, contextual, historical, and economic conditions that contribute to material and resource inequalities that negatively affect educational outcomes. For instance, research has consistently shown that parents of racially and ethnically diverse students with disabilities are often offered lower-quality services than their peers and that culturally and linguistically diverse parents are not as fully engaged in the special education advocacy process, as language and cultural barriers can dissuade their participation (e.g., Blue-Banning, Summers, Frankland, Nelson, & Beegle, 2004; Garcia, Mendez Perez, & Ortiz, 2000; Harry, 2002; Harry, Allen, & McLaughlin, 1995; Harry, Klingner, & Hart, 2005; Kalyanpur, Harry, & Skrtic, 2000; Kozleski et al., 2008). In addition, major misunderstandings between school personnel and families can lead to negative misperceptions, disregard, and disrespect toward culturally and linguistically diverse students and families (Harry, 2008; Harry et al., 2005; Kummerer & Lopez-Reyna, 2009). These dynamics constrain the process of opportunity hoarding because the connections and networks between school officials and families are weakened when parents are not fully included in the schooling process. Collectively, these social forces lead to consequential power imbalances that exist between families and schools and have major equity implications for how students are served.

In all three districts, the social forces associated with parental advocacy through IDEA, opportunity hoarding, and colorblindness had equity implications that affected how educational services were delivered to students. In Huntertown, parents used special education, and IDEA more generally, to secure resources for their children, without ever thinking about the equity implications of their actions. And the leaders and educators in the district seemed to support these practices, no matter what the cost. On the other hand, in Sunderville, parents and/or guardians were given very little agency to sway educators' decisions about how their children would be served and what educational services they would be given. IDEA was used in a race-neutral, technical, and decontextualized manner that negatively affected how educators, families, and students connected. In Gerrytown, the communication channels between parents and/or guardians and the school system were extremely fractured, and students' academic and social needs were lost in the cracks. There were no spaces or places where families and educators could meaningfully connect, and this affected how educational services were delivered to students in the district.

Huntertown: Parental "Power" in Action

Special education was highly sought after by parents in Huntertown. Parents, overwhelmingly white parents, often came to the district offices requesting admission into special education. I often sat in meetings where eligibility for special education was repeatedly requested and rarely denied.

This dynamic stressed out Cynthia. She consistently expressed to me during fieldwork that the "promises" of IDEA and the power given to parents through the legislation gave her "a lot of anxiety." She felt like she had to "always" accommodate parental requests, despite her professional expertise and opinion.

While in the field, I observed Cynthia repeatedly battling the threat of litigation from parents who were leveraging IDEA to secure educational resources for their children. Cynthia knew that once a child was classified, the law offered an abundance of services, and parents expected those services to be given to them immediately, or else. I often heard her say to her staff, "I don't play," when they would question why they had to accommodate parents so much. And, time after time, I observed Cynthia exhausting herself and her staff in meeting the needs and desires of families of students with disabilities.

For instance, while in the field I observed a meeting called by a white mother who had a daughter in special education. She was very upset about her daughter's state English test scores. The mother called the meeting because she wanted her daughter to receive more special education services from the district. The girl's tests scores were eight points below her previous year's score. Cynthia, the grade school principal, the girl's special education teacher, a speech pathologist, and I were at the meeting.

As we waited for the mother to arrive, I was struck by the silence among the professionals in the room. Everyone seemed strangely timid, and unwilling to speak to one another. Cynthia made it more awkward when the speech therapist in the room, whom I had not yet met, asked who I was. Cynthia replied, "She is someone who is going to write a book about us and how we are all racist." I began to explain that this was not the purpose of my research, but I was interrupted when the mother suddenly entered the room.

The mother immediately sat down, spread out three binders, pulled out numerous papers, and aggressively looked around the room. No one spoke as she organized her papers until Cynthia finally said, "Welcome." The greeting gave the mother the chance to begin.

She began by stating, "I called this meeting to advocate for my child." She continued, "Math used to be a problem for her, but now it seems like reading is, and her report card and ELA test [scores] are not good. She needs more special education services to help her." The mother shared that she had "paid a very expensive, well-known" neurologist, whom many parents in the district used, to assess her daughter. She told us to Google the doctor "because only very good things will come up when you search his name." She added, "I know what I am talking about," and proceeded to hand out copies of her daughter's ELA scores and pointed to the score drop. The table remained silent.

The mother continued, "My daughter is having trouble with inferences. Do you notice this too?" For the first time in the meeting, a professional (the special education teacher) decided to speak up: "Making inferences is a common skill students struggle with in the beginning of 4th grade because it involves more complex thinking." The speech teacher then added, "She is surpassing all of her speech goals and may not need speech [help] anymore." The special education teacher and the speech pathologist were trying to communicate to the mother that her daughter was performing well and could actually benefit from fewer services. The mother did not like this and immediately fought back.

About 20 minutes of back-and-forth discussion ensued until the mother said, "I don't want to come off obnoxious, but this form here [pointing to the state-generated ELA test score report] says that the school is required to help my daughter if she is below a certain level!" The mother added with increasing force, "What is the school going to do?" Cynthia aggressively entered the conversation at this point and assured the mother that the special education team would look at her daughter's IEP goals, address the mother's concerns, and stay in contact. Cynthia had to repeatedly remind the mother that the school was going to help the girl succeed.

The mother used her social and economic capital to influence the direction of the meeting. She also hoarded resources by aligning the mandates of IDEA, state testing guidelines, and a local community doctor who was often used by well-connected parents in the community, to demand that Huntertown School District cater to her needs. In the end, the mother got exactly what she wanted, more services for her daughter. Cynthia agreed that the school district would provide more, even though the professionals at the table did not think it was necessary. This meeting was not an anomaly; it was the norm.

Cynthia and her colleagues would often allow parents to run special education meetings and district staff would accommodate almost anything imaginable. I often felt exhausted after sitting in on IEP meetings because they were so time-consuming and labor-intensive for everyone involved. For instance, once I observed a 3-hour special education meeting where 2 of the 3 hours were dedicated to helping a girl labeled emotionally and behaviorally disturbed get into a history class that she wanted to take. The discussion was not centered on her disability and the course content; rather, it was centered on her desire to be in a different class. The girl's mother had brought along a "family friend who is also a lawyer" to help facilitate the requests. As it was midyear, the educators struggled to accommodate the girl's request because student schedules were already set. The amount of back-and-forth that ensued about the history class among the parent, student, staff, and administration was mind-boggling. However, at the conclusion of the meeting the child's desires were met and the professionals in the room accommodated her preferences.

Sometimes Cynthia, despite the exhaustion that attended her work with parents in the district, chose to over-accommodate parents who held an influential role in the school system. One special education meeting in particular illustrated this dynamic to me, and it was memorable too because of the time and emotional care Cynthia and her team put into it. The meeting was called by a white student's parents and occurred in the middle of the school year. The meeting's participants included Cynthia, the parents (who had strong connections to the school board), a school counselor, a special education teacher, a general education teacher, and me. The meeting lasted about an hour and it was very personal.

Throughout the meeting, it was obvious that Cynthia was invested in maintaining the parents' happiness and emotional comfort. For instance, about 5 minutes into the meeting, Cynthia told the parents, "Any time you are unhappy or feel uncomfortable, just call a special education meeting and we [the school] will fix the issue." The parents were grateful for the care and concern Cynthia expressed for their daughter.

The parents were concerned about their daughter, who has significant disabilities, and her bus ride to school in the morning. The bus matron refused to help their daughter buckle her seatbelt during the morning bus ride. Their daughter could not do it by herself because of her physical disabilities. The parents could not get on the bus because of the bus company's rules. And, when the matron was asked to help the girl, she would not do it because it was "not part of her job description." During the meeting, Cynthia found a way to make sure that the bus company cooperated with the parents' request so that their daughter was safe on her ride to school. The parents thanked her many times during the meeting.

Right before the meeting ended, Cynthia asked the parents if there was anything else she could do to help them. When she said this, she handed out a sheet of paper with a detailed description of the 13 disability categories that students can be classified with under IDEA. I had seen the form used in initial classification meetings, but rarely in one where the child was already classified as having "multiple disabilities."

As Cynthia handed out the paper she told the parents to "take it home, look over it," and "let me know if you [the parents] want to pick a new disability category for your daughter." As the mother took the form she asked, "If we change the label, will it change any of the services she receives?" Cynthia quickly answered, "No, it won't. And there is no rush. Just get back to me whenever you decide how you want your daughter to be labeled." Cynthia relinquished her professional opinions to cater to the parents. She asked the parents to choose a less stigmatizing category than "multiple disabilities," and suggested that the child be labeled with "something like other health impairment (OHI)" because, as she told me after the meeting, this was a much more "desirable" label to have.

While the content of the meeting was serious, the way in which Cynthia worked with the parents was extraordinary. Cynthia was well aware that the parents were powerful people embedded in the social context of

Huntertown. She knew that it was in her best interest to cater to their needs. However, by offering them a less stigmatizing disability label for their child, she effectively handed over her professional expertise in exchange for the parents' satisfaction. These kinds of interactions strengthened the demanding culture of parental involvement in the district.

Once, when Cynthia was preparing for a special education meeting for a young boy who had multiple severe disabilities incurred on school grounds in a fluke accident, she was interrupted by a call from the superintendent who demanded that she respond to a mother who was threatening litigation over an iPad that was given to her son.[1] While on the phone, Cynthia acted exasperated. When she got off, she looked at me and said, "You know, it's like, what is more important?" She shook one hand, raised it above her head and said, "This is the boy who has multiple disabilities who needs our help," and then shaking the other hand and again raising it above her head, said, "This is the need for an iPad2, not the iPad1, but the iPad2 because the boy is embarrassed to not have the latest technology!" She then shook both hands wildly and said again, "What is more important?" I distinctly remember looking at her as she dropped her head to her desk and said through a muffled voice caught in a stack of papers, "It's not about education . . . it's more about 'Hey, I want some of that, give it to me NOW!'" Cynthia had identified one of the greatest sources of tension in her work; by constantly responding to parents and catering to their needs, which she often had to do for legal reasons, she couldn't serve students the way she wanted to. In addition, the way that parents hoarded educational resources, and Cynthia's support of the process, ensured that both race and class inequalities would be maintained in the district, because individual needs were met but the aggregate effects of these decisions on an inequity like disproportionality were never examined.

Sunderville: Parental "Power" in Action

Lilla and her administrative team, like Cynthia in Huntertown, felt pressure to avoid litigation through IDEA from parents. However, the way in which Lilla, Marc, and Melinda approached this threat, and parents more generally, was radically different from the way Cynthia did in Huntertown. Rather than cater to parents' demands, Lilla and her administrative team tightly controlled the special education process as they desperately sought to achieve compliance with IDEA.

Marc told me that the outcomes of many special education meetings— whether IEP meetings, manifestation determination meetings, or annual reviews—were strategically discussed among staff before parents came to the table. Marc encouraged his staff to decide on an outcome for a meeting before it started, in order to control how educational resources were offered and delivered to students. The strategy was problematic for two reasons.

First, while it is important for a special education team to work together and problem-solve a child's issues, predetermining a meeting's outcome does not adequately welcome or incorporate parent input. Second, the strategy places technical language and bureaucratic compliance with IDEA at the forefront of district interactions with families, which limits meaningful parent and/or guardian participation and the process of opportunity hoarding. This didn't mean that parents and/or guardians were passive recipients of educational services; rather, they were closed out of conversations and opportunities to engage with educators because technical and impersonal policy language stifled interactions between school officials and families.

The technical use of IDEA and the focus on compliance in Sunderville was also enshrouded in a colorblind logic. Virtually none of the special education meetings I attended included conversations about the contextual factors that may be affecting a student's academic and/or behavioral performance. Rather, the meetings were run in a machine-like manner. The appropriate regulatory steps were taken and conclusions were made about a student's academic and behavioral needs based on the letter of the law. The colorblind, race, and context-neutral approach for using IDEA exacerbated inequalities and discipline disparities. These dynamics were clearly evident during a manifestation determination meeting I attended for a 17-year-old Black girl, Cindy, who had been repeatedly suspended throughout the school year. Her meeting is an example of just how little input and influence parents had on the special education process in Sunderville.

The meeting was held because Cindy had accumulated 10 out-of-school suspensions, which, through IDEA, requires that a manifestation determination meeting be held to determine if her behavior was the result of her disability or something else. The meeting's participants consisted of a meeting chair; a psychologist; Cindy's mother, who was on speakerphone; one of the student's teachers; and me. The meeting began when the mother came onto speakerphone and the chair stated the purpose of the gathering: "We are going to determine whether or not Cindy's suspensions are a result of her disability." The chair paused and then continued, "She [Cindy] has been suspended 10 times for the following: being out of supervision; cutting class; and insubordination." The chair listed Cindy's infractions as if she were reading a grocery list. The chair then proceeded to define Cindy's "insubordination":

> Insubordination for her means that she was in the ISS (in-school suspension) room and she wouldn't change her seat, she was in music class and she wouldn't change her seat, she cursed and walked out of a class, and she used inappropriate language while walking in the halls and was overheard by a teacher when this happened, and she was caught in hall sweeps. All together, she has accumulated 10 out-of-school suspensions.

After reading off the list of infractions, the chair looked up from her computer and sighed, "It's the typical bundle," referring to the types of suspensions Cindy had accrued. The chair also commented that she was used to having MDs (manifestation determinations) for special education students in which "these types" of infractions were common.

After the chair explained the offenses, she leaned into the phone and asked the mother if she had any questions. The mother responded, "Nope. I know about all these. She [Cindy] told me about them." The chair then looked back at her computer and started to read verbatim from her computer screen the rights of a student with a disability who has been suspended and the rationale for why the meeting was being held. When she finished, the mother's voice crackled through the speakerphone and said, "Yes, I know all these regulations." The chair then paused and looked at the people in the meeting and silently mouthed, "She [the mother] has been through this a lot." Some participants at the table appeared to silently laugh. The chair then gestured with her hands in a manner that seemed to encourage the table to begin speaking.

Suddenly, the team started a brief discussion about whether or not Cindy's disability was related to her infractions. Everyone at the table said a few words, and after this they all agreed that they did not think her disability was related to the nature of the infractions. This prompted the chair to summarize the findings of the participants' discussion and say, "OK, we have decided she [Cindy] was willfully disobeying school rules and thus the suspensions will stand as is." The chair then asked the mother if she had any questions, and the mother said she did not. The chair then ended the meeting by telling the mother that despite their determination, the team would consider creating a behavioral intervention plan (BiP) for Cindy and offer more counseling sessions as needed. The mother agreed to everything, and the chair ended the meeting with a click of a button on the phone. The educator's technical, matter-of-fact, and unquestionable presentation of the infractions and the regulations did not provide Cindy's mother with much room to object to the educators' recommendations. In addition, the educators justified Cindy's mother's silence by saying that she knew the regulations and the special education process.

When the mother was off the phone, the teacher at the table said, "I appreciate how we know the outcome of the meeting before it happens." The chair did not know that I knew of this practice, so she explained to me her understanding of it: "Administration, especially Marc, thought it would be best to predetermine the outcomes of these meetings before they occur so we are all on the same page." She added, "This way, it is difficult for anyone to sway the outcome of the meeting while it is occurring." As the chair was explaining how the MDs ran, Marc walked into the room and overheard our conversation. He added, "It's good for our budget to predetermine" the outcome before a meeting starts, and "I always tell chairs hold the line, strip services, shave down IEPs, and don't send kids to alternative settings!" Everyone chuckled and Marc went on, "It's how we make sure we are protecting the kids from unneeded services." The chair then explained to me that students in the district often received the "wrong" special education services because there was a history of noncompliance in the district, so this was their attempt to make sure that students receive the right educational services.

When the meeting adjourned, the chair and I lingered in the room. I asked her what she thought about Cindy's meeting and the "typical bundle" of suspensions she had accrued. The chair told me:

> The strategies we are asked to focus on, like BIPs, are ineffective. They are not the real solution or what is needed, but that is what we are pushed to do. I told Lilla this and suggested we bring in more support staff to help the kids, but Lilla says that they can't do it because of budget issues. I know Lilla has the students in the forefront of her mind and she is an amazing leader, but we aren't helping the kids.

The chair was referring to the fact that she felt very limited in what she could do to actually help a student like Cindy. She felt like she had to comply with IDEA, but that compliance did not guarantee that high-quality services or interventions were provided to students with disabilities in the district. She continued to muse about the meeting:

> I often wonder how so many kids can be sick so young [referring to the number of students who get suspended in the district]. We are just finding ways to warehouse the really sick kids [in special education], and then there are a bunch of middle-ground kids who can't be serviced well in the district or in an alternative education setting because we don't have the right services, and it makes me really sad. We just keep handing out the typical bundle [of infractions] . . . these suspensions are so predictable and cyclical, and then we are [asked] to create an FBA or a BIP but there are no alternatives and they [the district] need more options in the school . . .We are stuck in a cycle: suspension-MD-suspension-MD. It's sad. The system we have here only maintains the kids. It doesn't fix them.

Her comments highlight how technical compliance with IDEA did not and could not adequately address student needs in Sunderville. In Cindy's case, and as the chair expressed to me after the meeting, Cindy was not getting the services she needed. Rather, "Band-Aid" standardized solutions were provided for her (and other students in the district) and these solutions did not raise questions about some of the deeper issues that might have contributed to Cindy's high number of disciplinary infractions. For example, no one asked why her infractions were so predictable. And no one questioned what her relationships were like with adults in the district. Essentially, the administrative team's compliance-at-any-cost approach put pressure on the educators in Sunderville to use IDEA in ways that were not responsive to students and families in the district, and students suffered the most from this policy-to-practice approach.

Lastly, in controlling a meeting's outcome, the administrative team inadvertently ensured that colorblind and context-neutral norms shaped the tone and tenor of special education meetings as the educators in Cindy's meeting used IDEA in a very decontextualized manner. This approach does not sufficiently account for the shifting demographic context of Sunderville's schools and the growing racial and class tensions that were present in the district. The technical approach also erased the humanity behind the regulations. And, unfortunately, when the educators in Sunderville took this approach, inequitable outcomes associated with disproportionate disciplinary outcomes seemed to reoccur without an end in sight.

Gerrytown: Parental "Power" in Action

The educators in Gerrytown School District struggled to engage parents and sustain meaningful parent-to-school connections that supported equitable outcomes. This was due to very different reasons than in Sunderville, though, as the leadership structures in Gerrytown were not united around a cohesive vision, and there was little to no systemic coordination and/or uniformity in how policies and procedures were used across the district. Rather, the weak leadership structures in Gerrytown, coupled with the fragmented community context, fostered an organizational context and district climate where educators had little to no accountability to families and to the broader community. The ruptured links and networks between families and the school system inadvertently fractured and weakened the power parents could have when using IDEA to support their children and ensured that the individual benefits associated with opportunity hoarding were not even remotely possible.

My fieldwork observations constantly revealed that each district office, school building, or segment of professionals within the district operated in silos. This organizational configuration created a space where educators could act in highly discretionary ways when serving students and families because there were few, if any, clear messages from the central leadership team about what to prioritize when serving students in the district. The silos and the lack of a cohesive district mission and vision also allowed educators' deficit-based beliefs about families to flourish, and this negatively affected how educational services were delivered to students. For instance, district staff in Gerrytown tended to describe parents through a deficit lens. They had "multiple jobs," did "not speak English," were "transitory," and did not "care" about their child's education. These deficit-based perspectives affected how special education services were delivered to students, as district leaders and educators often provided the bare minimum to families and families were expected to accept it.

For example, one day during fieldwork I observed a series of eight special education meetings scheduled within a 3-hour period at a middle school. One meeting was memorable because it was illustrative of how parents were often treated in the district. The meeting was convened to discuss the case of a Latinx 6th-grade boy classified with an emotional and behavioral disorder. Roger (the district-level special education administrator), a special education teacher, a general education teacher, a social worker, a guidance counselor who was the boy's case manager, and I were in attendance.

The meeting began with the student arriving shortly after the bell rang. The professionals in the room welcomed him with a hello. He sat down next to me. Roger was on his computer and he did not look up from it when the boy sat down, but he did say hello as he continued to type on his computer. The other professionals in the room greeted the boy and then immediately got to business.

One by one, the educators began to give their academic and social–emotional reports on the student. They were all negative and spanned academic, social, and interpersonal issues. The student sat quietly through the first teacher's report, but midway through the second teacher's report, the boy asked, "Shouldn't my mother be present at this meeting?" His question spurred a considerable amount of confusion because no one could answer why she wasn't there.

The boy's question got Roger to look away from his computer and he looked visibly concerned. In that moment, Roger realized that the boy's mother was not present and he asked the boy what phone number he should call to get her on the phone. The boy gave him a phone number and Roger immediately got his mother on speakerphone.

When Roger said hello and explained to the mother why he was calling, she was surprised that a meeting was being held for her son. She said that she had not received a letter, or any notice, indicating that the special education meeting was going to happen. This is a violation of IDEA, as parents have to be notified whenever a meeting is convened about their child. Roger said he was unsure about why that happened and he apologized to her. He then asked the teachers in the room to continue giving their reports about the boy while he looked up the mother's contact information in the computer system.

While Roger worked on his computer and pulled up the family contact information, the professionals continued with their reports and the mother remained on the phone line, silent. One teacher said, "He is failing with a 40 average"; another reported, "It looks like he doesn't do work anywhere," referring to her class. With this comment, Roger stopped looking at his computer and asked the boy what was happening with him at school. He answered, "Nothing," and pulled his sweatshirt hood over his face. At this point, the mother began to talk very fast and with apparent frustration, going in and out of Spanish: "This is the first time I have ever heard that he was failing!" Two teachers quickly responded, almost in unison, "I sent letters home!" This prompted the boy's case manager to read aloud the boy's address she had on file, and both the mother and the son said it was incorrect. Roger stopped looking for the address on his computer and asked the mother for the correct address, which he then entered into his computer.

The negative reports continued after this exchange. The mother continued to remain relatively silent on the phone and it was uncomfortable. The teachers kept describing the student's academic and behavioral issues with negative and deficit-based language. It didn't stop until it became unbearable for Roger and he stopped the teachers from reading their reports. He leaned into the speakerphone and said to the mother, "You should come into the school and speak with his teachers. We need to increase the communication between home and school" to better support the student.

As the case manager started to go through the boy's schedule to see when they could coordinate a time for the mother to come in, the case manager offhandedly noted, "You know, he has been absent 22 times and late 61 times." The mother gasped and expressed disbelief over the phone. Roger asked the counselor and the boy's first-period teacher why they didn't notify his mother about his absences and tardiness. The teacher replied, "I send letters home all the time," while the counselor added, "I don't speak Spanish so I don't call home." I was immediately struck by her comment because the mother was primarily speaking English over the phone. The absurdity of the situation prompted Roger to state,

> For the record, I want everyone to know that these meetings can't be about parents first finding out about absences or latenesses. We are already into late March and parents should not be finding out at this point in the year that their child has been absent 22 days and late 61 times!

The teachers became defensive at this point, and Roger decided to end the meeting. He assured the mother that she would meet with the boy's case manager the next day in school. The mother was quiet, but said thank you and hung up the phone.

The events in this meeting were devastating to both the student and the mother. The boy had to advocate for himself and question why his mother wasn't present in the meeting. The educators in the room did not notice her absence, and if they did, they didn't acknowledge it until the boy said something. In addition, the way in which the mother was brought onto speakerphone and included in the meeting was problematic. She was treated as if she were inconsequential. She was also blamed for not responding to the teachers' letters that were sent home—to the wrong address—and to their attempted phone calls, which were made to the wrong number. The teachers never apologized for their lack of communication with the mother and with Roger. And lastly, the boy was in 6th grade, and no one had noticed, prior to this meeting, that he was consistently missing from school. His absences and latenesses were treated as an inconsequential fact that was discovered in the meeting. It was as if the educators in the room were so disconnected from one another, the boy, and his family that whatever happened to the boy would be OK because they would not be held accountable.

The failure of Roger, the caseworker, and the teachers in the room to notice that the boy was struggling in school, and their failure to communicate this to his mother, was a communication, professional, and organizational breakdown. Even though the lack of communication and oversight over the boy's educational trajectory was startling, it was illustrative of how public school parents were treated in the district; they weren't given much and they couldn't expect much in return. Not even IDEA compliance could pull the educators together in the room to adequately service the student's needs.

INDIVIDUAL REMEDIES FOR SYSTEMIC INEQUITIES

Parents and/or guardians are given a critical role in the IDEA implementation process. Unfortunately though, due to weak federal and state enforcement of IDEA regulations, parents have become the primary advocates for their children when interfacing with IDEA and school systems. But parents were not and are not meant to be one of the primary enforcement mechanisms for ensuring that the substantive and civil rights intents of IDEA are realized in educational practice because, ideally, LEA and SEA enforcement should have just as much of a positive impact on student outcomes as parental consent.

There are equity implications associated with the central role that parents play in the IDEA implementation process, because the educational system differentially rewards and responds to varying habitus, means of parental engagement, and social and cultural capital. And, when schools validate the social and cultural practices of dominant cultures, not all parents and/or guardians have equal opportunity and access to demand the educational resources that may be necessary for their children to succeed. This process is also encased within racial ideologies like colorblindness that naturalize, neutralize, and justify the resulting race and class inequalities that manifest.

The social forces that are associated with parental engagement and the social reproduction of inequality are exacerbated by the individualistic nature of IDEA legislation. McCall and Skrtic (2009), in their critique of disproportionality policy and IDEA, state that IDEA legislation represents an "atomization of needs politics," because disability policy is no longer concerned with a collective social justice agenda, but caters to individual needs and individual parental advocacy (p. 14). This atomization of needs politics diffuses the impact of inequality and reduces it to an individual issue. It also does not recognize that not all families have equal power vis-à-vis school systems to advocate for their children for a variety of social, contextual, historical, political, and economic reasons. Therefore, the un-intended consequences that are associated with the large role that parents have in the IDEA implementation process, coupled with the social forces that thwart equity and reproduce inequality, raise questions about just how effective compliance with IDEA can be when addressing an inequity like disproportionality. And most important, it again raises the central question that can be found throughout this book: When pursuing equity in special education, does compliance matter in special education?

CHAPTER 5

The Logic of Compliance

There is a deeply troubling social justice problem that exists at the intersection of the guarantee of a free appropriate public education for students with disabilities and the persistence of racial inequities in special education. Artiles (2011) outlines the contours of this problem and paradox by stating, "the civil rights response for one group of individuals (i.e., learners with disabilities) has become a potential source of inequities for another group (i.e., racial minority students) despite their shared histories of struggle for equity" (p. 431). Understanding why the civil rights response for students with disabilities has been unsuccessful in securing equal educational opportunity and access for culturally, racially, linguistically, and ethnically diverse learners in special education requires deep sensitivity to the historical, political, economic, and social factors that influence the delivery of educational services to all students across the United States. It also requires understanding theoretically how the technical and procedural focus of IDEA relates to its civil rights intent and to persistent racial inequities in special education.

CIVIL RIGHTS INTENT AND PROCEDURAL COMPLIANCE

In order to understand why and how legal compliance with IDEA—a civil rights–based piece of legislation—can coexist with persistent racial inequities in special education, the logic of compliance has to be examined. This can be done by using the insights of neo-institutional theory, which, broadly speaking, is a theoretical perspective that examines how policy and legal mandates shape organizations and influence the people working within them (e.g., DiMaggio & Powell, 1983; Edelman, 1990; Meyer & Rowan, 1977). Neo-institutional theory places the legal and policy environment that surrounds an organization—or, in this case, schools—at the forefront of theoretical and empirical inquiry as it examines how social structures, norms, rules, and broader organizational cultures shape and/or constrain an

*Portions of this chapter are taken from the following article: Kramarczuk Voulgarides, C., Fergus, E., & King Thorius, K. A. (2017). Pursuing equity: Disproportionality in special education and the reframing of technical solutions to address systemic inequities. *Review of Research in Education, 41*(1), 61–87.

individual's agency. In relationship to schools, it acknowledges that the legal and policy environment affects the delivery of education just as much as the ecological context does (Arum, 2000).

Lauren Edelman, in her study on compliance with Equal Employment Opportunity (EEO) and affirmative action law (1992), used neo-institutional theory to highlight how procedurally dense, yet legally ambiguous, civil rights laws can be complied with despite a lack of positive results. Edelman's use of neo-institutional theory provides analytical insight into the connections between IDEA implementation, its civil rights intent, and persistent racial inequities in special education. For one thing, Edelman (1992) states that when laws have a "procedural emphasis," it is very difficult for outside authorities and/or agencies to detect discrimination that is not blatantly obvious. This is because compliance with organizational procedures symbolically signals nondiscriminatory behavior. In relation to IDEA, the legislation is procedurally dense and compliance oriented, regulating organizational procedures more so than the substantive results of those procedures. The legislation's foundational premise is also legally ambiguous, vague, and hard to legislate—centered on ensuring equal opportunity and the promise that all students receive a free appropriate public education (FAPE). FAPE has never been clearly defined or outlined in the legislation, and its meaning continues to be contested in the U.S court system. Second, Edelman states that when a law has "weak enforcement mechanisms" that provide "inadequate and inconsistent feedback on what organizational practices are legal" (p. 1539), then the organization has a significant amount of discretion to use law in a way that is responsive to the local context, norms, and ways of being rather than toward achieving a civil rights outcome. In relationship to special education, actual enforcement of IDEA and subsequent sanctions are minimal from federal and state education agencies, especially with respect to disproportionality (e.g., Albrecht et al., 2012; Cavendish et al., 2014; Skiba, 2013). Edelman (1992) also describes how "structural elaboration," which refers to the way in which organizations react to their environments and strategically implement formal structures to signal conformity with institutional norms, allows for an organization to meet its own interests and simultaneously remain socially legitimate (compliant). Essentially, structural elaboration is related to the organizational gap that exists between the formal offices, positions, and rules of an organization and the informal norms and ways of being of an organization. It allows for managers to maintain some control over their workflow and maintain the legitimacy of the organization without radically changing their practices as they show procedural compliance with civil rights mandates. The concept implies that it is much easier for people within organizations to symbolically comply (Meyer & Rowan, 1977) with policy mandates, rather than shift their organizational culture and norms as they show compliance with a civil rights mandate.

Collectively, these factors lead to the presence of legal endogeneity (Edelman, Krieger, Eliason, Albiston, & Mellema, 2011). Legal endogeneity implies that courts, governing bodies, and other actors involved in the legal process take evidence of organizational structures as proof of compliance with the intent of the law (Edelman et al., 2011). Legal endogeneity is problematic because if organizational structures, policies, rules, handbooks, and the like are relied upon as evidence of compliance with civil rights law, the law's effectiveness is weakened (Edelman et al., 2011). And the substantive content of a law and/or policy is lost when organizational and procedural structures are taken for granted as evidence of compliance with civil rights concerns.

For instance, in relationship to special education, the presence of a completed IEP does not ensure that the legislation has been substantively applied to practice or that all educational opportunities have been exhaustively offered to, or provided for, a student. However, a correctly filled out IEP does illustrate proof of compliance with IDEA, and proof that educational opportunity was given to a student via the very existence of the document. The IEP, if all its "i's" are dotted and all its "t's" are crossed, is proof enough that educators have done their job. Legal endogeneity does not and cannot ensure that students receive the best educational services possible.

Therefore, the logic of compliance—characterized by procedurally dense and legally ambiguous laws, structural elaboration, symbolic compliance, and legal endogeneity—undermines equity, because when educators work in schools and districts that are found to be disproportionate, yet can show compliance with IDEA, it implies that educators are faithfully applying the law and adhering to the principles of equal educational opportunity and access. It does not engage with the possibility that: (1) educators may be explicitly or implicitly discriminating against students of color; (2) the local context affects how educational services are delivered to students; and (3) students may be erroneously placed in special education and/or excessively disciplined. The logic of compliance also does not account for the organizational and policy pressures that subvert the best intentions of people, policies, and practices. Most problematically, the logic of compliance fuels deficit-based beliefs about individuals, because under this logic educators are doing all they can to ensure that students receive a free appropriate public education. And, because disproportionality is often framed as a technical issue that can be "fixed" through policy interventions and/or programs, if students are not succeeding, it implies that it is their fault. This has implications for how the educational interventions embedded in IDEA relate to educators' efforts to address disproportionality in special education.

SOLVING DISPROPORTIONALITY THROUGH THE LOGIC OF COMPLIANCE

Although the 1997 and 2004 reauthorizations of IDEA recognize that racial disparities have plagued the U.S. special education system for decades, the actual compliance remedies associated with addressing disproportionality do not—and were not designed to—substantively engage with the complex factors that contribute to disproportionate outcomes in special education. Rather, compliance monitoring for disproportionality is reliant upon LEAs and SEAs adhering to procedural remedies that, when complied with, symbolically or substantively, signify that equal opportunity and access have been provided to *all* students. This has contributed to a logic of compliance, wherein organizational structures, policies, and procedures have been used as evidence of compliance with civil rights concerns.

For example, the policy interventions and/or programs that are designed to address the needs of students with disabilities, and that are often used in districts and schools that are suffering from disproportionality, are centered upon remedying individual students rather than systematically interrogating how social norms, context, culture, and social structures contribute to disparate racial outcomes in special education. Two widely used interventions, Response to Intervention (RtI) and Positive Behavioral Interventions and Supports (PBIS), both of which are a form of Multi-Tiered System of Supports (MTSS) (Averill & Rinaldi, 2011; Jimerson, Burns, & VanDerHeyden, 2016; Kuchle, Zumeta Edmonds, Danielson, Peterson, & Riley-Tillman, 2015), do not, and cannot, sufficiently address disproportionate outcomes because of their decontextualized and individual approaches for addressing student needs. In other words, they do not sufficiently engage with the effects of culture and context on educational outcomes. This is despite the fact that they are validated interventions embedded in the most recent reauthorization of IDEA and that many state education departments encourage their use to address inequities in special education.[1]

RtI emerged within the special education research community in the early 2000s in response to a commission by the U.S. Congress that convened to discuss issues in special education (Finn, Rotherham, & Hokanson, 2001). While there is considerable variability in how RtI frameworks have been operationalized in educational practice, there are several key premises upon which all RtI frameworks are grounded. These include prevention of school failure, reliance on curriculum-based measurements of students' progress to determine the need for academic and/or social interventions, and a focus on the early application of interventions to help students succeed (Thorius, Maxcy, Macey, & Cox, 2014).

Several researchers and policymakers have expressed hope in the potential for RtI to address the disproportionate representation of culturally, racially, ethnically, and linguistically diverse students in special education, because the framework assesses students' needs much earlier in the schooling process and it requires a redistribution of high-quality opportunities to learn (e.g., Artiles, Bal, & Thorius, 2010). However, researchers have also cautioned that such approaches must account for the multilayered and nuanced understandings of culture that shape how RtI is conceptualized and enacted in local contexts (Artiles, 2015; Thorius, Maxcy, Macey, & Cox, 2014) as concerns about the impact of RtI on disproportionality continue to mount (e.g., Artiles, 2015).

For instance, in 2010, McKinney, Bartholomew, and Gray found patterns of racial and linguistic student overrepresentation in RtI's second and third tiers. Bouman (2010) found that the number of African American students labeled with specific learning disabilities (SLD), under an RtI framework implemented in California, actually increased over a 5-year period despite the overall reduction of students eligible for SLD support across all racial groups combined. PBIS has a similar relationship with disproportionate outcomes.

Over the past 10 years, Positive Behavior Interventions and Supports (PBIS) have become a prominent strategy for addressing disparate disciplinary outcomes in schools and districts. PBIS uses a multi-tiered systems approach, like RtI, to proactively and positively address discipline in schools (Mrazek & Haggerty, 1994; Walker et al., 1996) by focusing on systematic and consistent use of active student supervision, providing positive feedback to students, and providing social skills instruction. Studies on the effectiveness of PBIS have shown that rates of problem behaviors appear to decrease with the implementation of the intervention (e.g., Colvin, Sugai, Good, & Lee, 1997; Heck, Collins, & Peterson, 2001; Kartub, Taylor-Greene, March, & Horner, 2000; Leedy, Bates, & Safran, 2004; Lewis, Colvin, & Sugai, 2000; Lewis, Sugai, & Colvin, 1998; Nelson, Colvin, & Smith, 1996; Putnam, Handler, Ramirez-Platt, & Luiselli, 2003). In addition, functional behavior assessments (FBAs) and behavioral intervention plans (BIPs), which are part of the multitiered continuum of interventions in PBIS, have also demonstrated a positive impact on the functioning of students with serious problem behaviors (Fairbanks, Sugai, Guardino, & Lathrop, 2007; Ingram, Lewis-Palmer, & Sugai, 2005; Moreno & Bullock 2011; Newcomer & Lewis, 2004). However, despite PBIS's general promise as a method for making school discipline more efficient and less exclusionary, there is little to no evidence about whether or not PBIS is effective in addressing racial disproportionality. In addition, there is some evidence that it may actually exacerbate the issue.

For example, Skiba, Horner, et al. (2011) explored patterns of office disciplinary referrals in a nationally representative sample of 364 elementary and middle schools that had been implementing schoolwide PBIS for at least one year. When the data were disaggregated across the national sample, Black and Latinx students were more likely than white students to receive a suspension or expulsion for minor infractions despite the use of the intervention system. And, outside of theoretical reviews concerning what a culturally responsive PBIS and intervention system might look like (e.g., Kozleski, Sobel, & Taylor, 2003; Utley, Kozleski, Smith, & Draper, 2002), one of the few empirical investigations of a culturally responsive model of PBIS is the Jones, Caravaca, Cizek, Horner, and Vincent (2010) study of the adaptation of a schoolwide PBIS for an elementary school serving Navajo students. Although the preliminary results of incorporating Diné language, culture, and history into one school's PBIS implementation structure suggested a substantial decrease in the overall rate of office disciplinary referrals, it is difficult to infer outward from a single case study.

These findings, coupled with those regarding RtI, suggest that the interventions may actually contribute to racial inequities rather than ameliorate them. In relation to this point, Sullivan, Artiles, and Hernandez-Saca (2015) state that special education interventions "may have been misconceived in foci" as they are "too molecular to affect the other interconnected and distal forces that drive disproportionality" (p. 131). And, when educators rely upon the use of technical decontextualized educational interventions to address a complex issue like disproportionality, it is unlikely that racial inequities can be addressed through compliance.

In Sunderville, Gerrytown, and Huntertown, disproportionality was addressed through the logic of compliance. In both Sunderville and Gerrytown, the special education district leaders relied upon PBIS, and FBAs and BIPs more specifically, to address disproportionality. However, the interventions were ineffective in reducing discipline disparities because they were symbolically applied to practice. In Huntertown, compliance was not at the forefront of district work, and this gave Cynthia and her staff the confidence that they were providing equal opportunity and access to all students in the district, despite the presence of disproportionality. And, even though state auditors had a consistent presence in the three districts, they did not have significant oversight of everyday district actions. Thus, in all three districts, the educators, intentionally or not, were able to use compliance with the legislation to signal adherence to the civil rights intent of IDEA. This made it very difficult for state auditors to find evidence of behavior that denied educational opportunity to some students over others because evidence of efforts to address disproportionality were reduced to one-dimensional compliance assessments. This is problematic, because as Artiles, Kozleski, Trent, Osher, and Ortiz (2010) state, "the reluctance to frame disproportionality as a *problem* [emphasis added] stresses technical arguments that ignore the role of historical, contextual, and structural forces" (p. 281), which in turn ultimately affects how the legislation is used and how the civil rights intent of the legislation is either realized—or thwarted—in educational practice.

Sunderville: Hypercompliant, Persistently Disproportionate

Sunderville School District had been under state oversight for years. Prior to Marc and Lilla's arrival in the district, there was not a consistent leader in the special education department. The lack of leadership allowed for compliance monitoring of IDEA to fall to the wayside. Several years of neglect left the district's files in disarray and the staff was largely unaccustomed to focusing on compliance with IDEA in practice. This reality was in direct contrast with the superintendent's incessant desire for the special education department to be in compliance with IDEA—immediately.

Dr. Lovene, the superintendent, specifically hired Lilla because of her reputation for turning around struggling special education departments in nearby school districts. Marc served as Lilla's self-described "foot soldier" and "hit man" for ensuring that compliance with IDEA was realized in practice. Marc said that in his first year in the district, he was able to "fix all of the noncompliance issues" associated with the citation and identified by the state "in a few months." He said that the state auditor who monitored the district's actions "appreciated" how swiftly the district had become compliant and that "he [the state auditor] had never seen a district become compliant so fast" after being cited.

When I first arrived in the district, Marc told me I could talk to "anyone and everyone" about the district's citation and disproportionality: "It [the citation] is very public knowledge" and "it is announced on the district's website." Marc was right in his assessment; knowledge of the citation was widespread and so well known among the educators in the district that I often found that they expressed a slight indifference to it. For instance, a district psychologist told me, "We constantly get data about what we're doing wrong, what we're bad at," adding, "I'm not surprised at all that we were cited. You kind of expect it." Staff members were generally accustomed to working under the assumption that the district was "doing wrong on something," as one teacher told me; however, despite this they were very frustrated by Marc's insistence that they rapidly become compliant with IDEA.

For instance, one building administrator I spoke with told me that he thought the special education department was forcing compliance "just to be compliant." A teacher I spoke with readily admitted that he thought that compliance was "pushed" on him and that it was detrimental to his educational practice. An elementary school teacher told me she felt as though she could not alter or adapt policies or procedures to the realities of her classroom; she felt like she had to do exactly what the administration told her to do in terms of technical compliance with IDEA, and sometimes it "just didn't make sense" to her. She also added that she knew she shouldn't suspend kids, but she felt very strongly that a system like PBIS, a BIP, or an FBA would not solve the disciplinary issues that she saw in her classroom and heard about in classrooms across the district.

A middle school principal clearly explained to me how the tensions surrounding compliance with IDEA affected him:

> People feel like they are walking on eggshells [when disciplining a student]. . . . You know, Marc . . . his answer to everything is "We'll write a check" [referring to incentive structures embedded in BIPs and FBAs], but you understand that every time a kid walks by somebody, he says 'f--k you' or something like that or whatever, and that's not acceptable anywhere, but we let them do it because we can't suspend? How is this BIP better? How will it fix the situation?

The principal was frustrated that the only tools he felt like he was armed with to address discipline issues were policies and procedures that did not seem relevant to his practice, to students, or to the needs of his classroom. The principal continued, "People [teachers], they throw in the towel because they're afraid to get in trouble [with the administration] or they're afraid of writing a kid up and getting back the write-up [from Marc that says], like 'Oh, look at the BIP first [before the teacher reacts].'" He added, "I'm trying to teach in a classroom where kids just say 'f—k you' in front of 30 of my students, and I'm supposed to say, you know, it's OK?" He was clearly frustrated with the fact that he had to push his teachers to comply with IDEA even though these acts of compliance didn't help them create a safe and productive classroom environment.

There were a few staff members who refrained from critiquing the special education administrative team. They were either closely aligned with Dr. Lovene or they were one of the select allies of Lilla and her administrative team. These staff members offered positive comments about compliance monitoring that were personalized. For example, a special education meeting chair praised Marc for his "keen eye" for identifying areas of noncompliance and Lilla was lauded for her "determination" to get Sunderville in compliance. However, the majority of staff members were bothered by it.

Periodically, Marc would express to me that he knew compliance was not the answer to the district's problems. However, he felt as though he had no other strategy for addressing disproportionality because "the state is only interested in compliance," and Dr. Lovene wanted the special education department to be in compliance with IDEA. Once, while I was sitting in Marc's office and we were discussing a student who was having disciplinary issues, he said, "I don't understand how a BIP will get a kid to come to school that doesn't want to come to school," but "following compliance measures is the only thing I have control over." He added, "The law limits what I can do, but I have to follow the law." Marc felt constrained by state pressure and oversight, the expectations that Dr. Lovene set around compliance, and the options afforded to him through IDEA to address disciplinary issues in Sunderville.

Lilla was not blind to the tensions surrounding compliance either. She knew that focusing on compliance upset her staff. However, when she acknowledged the frustrations the staff had, she often framed the administrative team's focus on compliance as a way "to get the needs of the kids to be first and foremost in everyone's mind." She would often invoke the spirit of IDEA and say that students had a right to receive the services entitled to them through the law—something that compliance was supposed to ensure. While I understood her logic, which was that the law was there to protect students with disabilities and provide educational services to them, my observations suggested that focusing on compliance was a double-edged sword. Instead of compliance protecting all students with disabilities in Sunderville, it often further alienated educators from the students they struggled to connect with the most. Additionally, the focus on compliance did not push staff to substantively engage with or be responsive to the changing demographics of the student body. Rather, staff focused on following a procedure or practice exactly as it was written because this is what administration wanted from them, and this often had negative consequences on student outcomes.

When Marc found out the district would be cited again for the 2012–2013 school year, he was ready to "finesse the files" and "triage" which ones he thought the state would target in order to ensure the district remained in full regulatory compliance with IDEA when addressing disproportionality. He admitted that he thought the compliance process was "all a horse-and-pony show," yet he felt obligated to "finesse the files" because it was expected of him. He told me that he felt like maintaining compliance was "great for me as a supervisor because I can fix little things, but it doesn't get to the root of the problem." He believed the root of the problems in Sunderville, and a contributor to disproportionality, were the "deep-seated tensions" in the community surrounding issues of race and class, but the bulk of his workflow wasn't focused on substantively addressing those issues.

Essentially, Marc's workflow was focused on ensuring that compliance was met at any cost. He put pressure on his staff to complete FBAs and BIPs even though the interventions did not meet the needs of students or the adults teaching them. Rather, they frustrated staff and hindered teaching and learning. Marc was rewarded for taking this approach toward compliance, though, by his superintendent and by the state auditor who monitored the district's efforts to address disproportionality. However, both Marc and Lilla knew that the interventions they pushed their staff to use were insufficient for addressing disproportionality. But the pressure to comply coming from state auditors, the superintendent, professional and moral obligations, and the historical context of the special education department in Sunderville ensured that the logic of compliance would dominate how educators interfaced with IDEA. And, even though procedural compliance with IDEA implied that the educators in the district were adhering to the principles of equal educational opportunity and access found in IDEA, many of the educators in the district knew this wasn't necessarily true, but they still complied because they had to. Compliance would be met at any cost, even if it negatively affected students and educators.

Gerrytown: Interventions and More Interventions

Gerrytown was also affected by the logic of compliance, but in a different way from Sunderville. Roger was extremely focused on adopting programs and/or interventions that would show compliance with IDEA to state auditors, even if they were not faithfully applied to practice. Compliance with IDEA, whether it was symbolic or not, also served as Roger's attempt to address disproportionality and unite educators around a common set of practices within the fragmented organizational context of the district. Disproportionality became a technical issue that could be addressed through policy interventions and/or programs.

Roger had worked in Gerrytown for several years prior to my arrival and he had extensive experience responding to the state's mandates surrounding a citation for disproportionality. Prior to my arrival in the district, Roger and his department had initiated a review of the district's special education policies, practices, and procedures in an attempt to remedy the department's compliance deficiencies. Roger told me his compliance efforts resulted in "a good relationship" with the state compliance auditor who monitored the district. The auditor had praised Roger for having "the right mentality" when addressing disproportionality.

Although Roger was relatively proactive in trying to address disproportionality, he was organizationally constrained by the central leadership team. Roger often told me that he did not think that they, the central leadership team, felt the same urgency to address disproportionality as he did. This became evident to me when I attended a cabinet meeting where the district's citation was discussed. The meeting consisted of the business director for the district; the human resources director; Dr. Gerald, the district's superintendent; the superintendent for curriculum; the assistant superintendent for curriculum; an outside consultant brought in to help the district understand their citation; Roger; and me.

The meeting began with the cabinet members sitting down in an office in the central administration building. The attendees were casually chatting about lunch plans and acupuncture when, after about 10 minutes of banter, Roger decided to start the meeting. He handed out a piece of paper to everyone in the room and said, "I received a Christmas present from the state—we will be cited this year for suspensions" for Black students with disabilities. Roger passed around a copy of an email he received from the state education department indicating that the district was being cited for disproportionality.

Dr. Gerald briefly looked at the paper and then at Roger and said, "Oh yes, we already know that. The 10th grade is really an issue this year." Dr. Katrina, the superintendent of curriculum, added, "The 10th-grade class has always been an issue." Both Dr. Gerald and Dr. Katrina spoke confidently as they pinpointed the source of the citation to a specific grade. They did not question whether or not the suspensions were legitimate or if larger systemic issues were contributing to their frequency, especially for Black students.

Roger looked upset by their comments. He did not engage with their statements, but rather stated, "The district will probably have to go under another comprehensive review by the state," referring to an IDEA compliance audit. Roger then handed out another piece of paper to everyone at the table. The handout had a list of all of the students who had been suspended up until the day of the meeting, along with their infractions. In the data, the 10th grade was equally implicated, as were other grades.

The cabinet members leafed through the suspension list in relative silence until the director of human resources, Dr. Seria, who was sitting next to Dr. Gerald, punctured the sound of the paper-turning with a chuckle: "I'm surprised we didn't get on the [citation] list earlier. We have two more [suspensions] to add to it today!" Pointing to the list, Dr. Gerald turned to Dr. Seria and said, "Oh, wow, they are already here!" With this, the district's business director, Dr. Arthur, pointed to the list of suspensions and looked at Roger and asked, "What are we supposed to do with this information?" Dr. Gerald followed up with a flat statement, "The district really has limited ability with money, so we really need to focus our resources," implying that addressing suspensions was not a top priority for the cabinet team.

Suddenly, the assistant superintendent of curriculum, Dr. Jones, who had been mostly silent, said, "You know if we can't pinpoint the problem [where the suspensions are coming from], then we can't address it." She was referring to the fact that if Roger could not tell the team why kids weren't behaving, then the district couldn't do anything about it. Dr. Katrina followed up after her statement and added, "How do we sweep this problem away and only this problem? We don't have time for anything else! Where is the broom to get rid of this?" Roger responded, "I think there are bigger issues contributing to the high number of suspensions in the district," but despite his comment, Dr. Katrina continued to inquire where the "broom" was to "sweep" away the problem. No one in the meeting was startled by the citation or wondered why disproportionality persisted in the district. And, despite Roger pushing the cabinet members to think beyond the 10th-grade class as the problem, the team consistently fell back on superficial solutions to address this complex issue.

Compounding the issue was that schools in Gerrytown operated in silos, islands unto themselves. There were few, if any, central administration directives that united the school buildings in the district. Roger was reactive to this reality and he incessantly focused on trying to adopt programs and/ or interventions that would show compliance with IDEA to state auditors in his efforts to address disproportionality. This was despite any evidence that the programs were effective or that they would be implemented with fidelity in schools across the district.

For instance, when Gerrytown was first cited for disproportionality, Roger immediately responded by hiring a special education behavior consultant to help address the lack of behavioral interventions (e.g., PBIS, FBA, BIP) in the district. The consultant had been working in the district for several years when I interviewed her and she was highly critical of how the district approached discipline. She told me that although she was "trained to look at the behavior of students comprehensively," she could not do this in Gerrytown. She had to do "things that felt unnatural" because Roger and the state auditors made it feel like the district had to "fix the problem [disproportionality] in the moment." She added, "All of my training on how to holistically understand a student doesn't matter here because this is a district that responds to the state." The compliance pressures she felt from Roger made her feel ineffective and unable to do her job. They also alienated her from the students she was hired to serve because compliance was a means to an end. It was not a method to ensure that educational opportunities were provided to all children.

The specific compliance remedies outlined in IDEA for Indicator 4 that focus on FBAs and BIPs, coupled with Roger's attempts to streamline district activities, put a considerable amount of compliance pressure onto the work of school psychologists, too. Psychologists are often required to design FBAs and BIPs, and Roger made sure that they were properly trained to do so. The psychologists went on numerous "FBA and BIP trainings," as one psychologist called it. I even attended one because they occurred so frequently while I was conducting fieldwork. However, despite the psychologists' training and the intense pressure to speedily create and implement FBAs and BIPs, there were few, if any, substantive changes made to educational practice that improved student outcomes.

One day I attended a psychologist PD where 20 minutes of the meeting were dedicated to learning about computer shortcuts that could be used when filling out an IEP. When Roger got to the part where FBA and BIP information should be entered into the computer system, he asked the psychologists, "How are the BIPs and FBAs coming along?" The room was silent for quite a while until one psychologist said, "Every time we hear 'FBA' or 'BIP,' we want to curl up into a ball and withdraw to the fetal position." Another added that they were "laborious" to create and that they weren't used properly in practice.

According to the psychologists, teachers did not consistently and appropriately implement the BIPs and/or FBAs they created. And, if teachers did use them, according to one psychologist, it was "for the wrong reasons." The behavior consultant, who was also in the meeting, explained, "I think teachers just want a BIP because they get annoyed with a kid. . . . Teachers always want to 'BIP' a kid" for "stupid things like he [the student] won't stop moving his foot!" The psychologist added, "I try to guide teachers to realize that [a student shaking his foot] is not a BIP-worthy behavior," but "my efforts are in vain because everyone in the district has to create a BIP here." She was referring to the fact that BIPs and FBAs had little to no meaning in the district. They were just another intervention and/or strategy that the educators had to symbolically comply with. They would do it, comply, but it didn't mean that it would shift their educational practice to better serve students. Essentially, FBAs and BIPs became part of the problem; they were a quick fix to deeper problems stemming from the community context, organizational culture of the district, and the need to comply with IDEA.

In one PD, a psychologist made a sarcastic comment about the effectiveness of FBAs and BIPs and the resources and collaboration needed to effectively implement them. She said, "Oh, are we talking about communicating with each other now?" referring to how teachers and psychologists are supposed to coordinate resources in order to implement the interventions. She added, "You mean we are trying to coordinate things to help those people? The kids?! In the buildings? We are trying to help them?!?" She sarcastically pointed out the immense gap that existed between what educators were supposed to do and what they actually did. While no one had an answer to her comment, I felt as if everyone understood the gravity of what she was implying: The hours of PD spent on learning to create a good-looking FBA or BIP had little effect on student outcomes. Clearly, staff needed more training on FBAs and BIPs, but, more problematically, the focus on compliance limited a practitioner's ability to substantively engage with localized inequities through the implementation of an FBA or a BIP.

Each time concerns like these were brought up by the psychologists, who were Roger's allies in the district, Roger did not seem to know how to handle their comments and he largely ignored them. The comments actually frustrated Roger because he directed a lot of time and energy to ensuring that his staff had access to professional development opportunities that were related to IDEA mandates. However, the trainings never translated to practice in a way that changed student outcomes, because in Gerrytown, superficial and symbolic compliance with IDEA was an accomplishment in and of itself in such a fragmented and disjointed context. And the logic of compliance permitted Roger and his staff to maintain some control over their workflow and maintain the legitimacy of the organization without ever having to radically shift their practices as they showed procedural compliance with IDEA.

Huntertown: Compliance is Equality and Equity

In Huntertown, the logic of compliance was dominated by legal endogeneity. The district did not have pervasive compliance issues like Sunderville, and Cynthia did not focus on establishing multiple educational interventions like Roger did in Gerrytown. Rather, the district's record of procedural compliance with IDEA was taken for granted as evidence of compliance with civil rights concerns. Compliance signaled to state auditors that the educators in the district faithfully adhered to the principles of equal educational opportunity and access. The district's record of compliance with IDEA also did not sufficiently raise state auditors' concerns that maybe some students in the district might be receiving lower-quality educational services compared to others or that educators may be explicitly or implicitly discriminating against students of color. Rather, the district's capacity to be in regulatory compliance with IDEA was evidence enough that the educators in Huntertown provided equal access and opportunity to high-quality educational services to *all* students in the district. This reasoning, stemming from the logic of compliance, influenced how Cynthia and her staff related to their citation for disproportionality.

Cynthia was very passionate about her job and frustrated by the citation and the state auditors who monitored her district. She thought the citation implied "negative and untrue things" about Huntertown. Cynthia would often tell me that Huntertown was a small district and it was "frustrating" to get cited because "one Black family could move in or out of the district" and that could determine whether or not the district was cited for Indicator 9. Cynthia faulted the state's formula for detecting disproportionality (significant disproportionality) as being inappropriate for small districts because numbers "get skewed and interpreted wrong." In my first phone conversation with Cynthia, where we talked about my coming to her district and shadowing her, she told me, "I want you to come here [to Huntertown] so I can prove to you the district is not doing wrong. We don't have a problem," implying that the special education department and the district did not have a legitimate issue with disproportionality. Her staff echoed similar sentiments.

I often spoke with staff members who didn't think there were any racial issues in the district either. For instance, one staff member told me that being "cited" was "really a numbers game." Another district employee said, "If one Black family moves in or out [of Huntertown], they [the state] got us!" Another staff member told me that there was very little racial diversity in the district, so he "couldn't understand how race could be a problem" in Huntertown when referring to the citation. Cynthia and her staff found ways to talk around the citation and not take ownership over what it implied—that discriminatory practices may have been occurring in her district.

Cynthia and her staff often used the phrase "Indicator 9, Indicator fine" to express their relationship with and understanding of the citation. Cynthia told me that the phrase captured how easily the district could be cited for disproportionality. When the district received an initial referral for special education for a Black child, she and the guidance counselor, in particular, questioned whether or not the child would be classified for special education. If they were, the district would be "Indicator 9" because the student would "push" them over the numerical threshold for disproportionality; if not, they would be "Indicator fine." The phrase was mostly used by special education staff and was often said with humor, a groan, or some flippancy. The phrase, and the way her staff talked about disproportionality, also dehumanized the implications of the citation and exonerated Cynthia and her staff from having any role in contributing to the inequity.

One day while I was sitting in Cynthia's office, the high school's director of counseling entered and asked Cynthia to sign a form. While Cynthia was doing so, she looked at me and said, "Indicator 9! Going to a residential center!" (a private out-of-district placement that takes the child off the district's special education roster). The counselor added, "Every one helps that we can get out!" referring to the fact that the Black student would no longer be on the district's rolls, thereby reducing the probability that Huntertown would be cited again for disproportionality. The exchange revealed how Cynthia and her staff rarely saw the district's systems, norms, cultural context, teachers, leaders, interventions, mindsets, and/or instructional practices as contributing to the issue.

Cynthia also felt like she did not have to prove to the state that she and her staff were complying with IDEA. She found the notion of procedural compliance offensive, especially in relationship to the state auditor's review of her district's policies, practices, and procedures associated with a citation for Indicator 9. Cynthia would often lament that the state auditor's process for finding issues of noncompliance was a "stupid little job." I would repeatedly hear her say things like "the stupidity of the process" or that the district's review was "frustrating" or "punitive" rather than helpful. Cynthia described her experience with the self-review when the state came "looking for issues" in Huntertown:

> You should have seen it! They [the state auditors] came here. You should have seen it. We had files [student IEP files] laid out all over the tables in here [her office], and the state picked 30 randomly, and they were digging, looking, searching for issues in the files.
> . . . There was nothing wrong with our files! They [the state] were looking for gaps on the things that don't really matter. . . . I felt like the state was being rude, belittling, [and] rolling their eyes at us.

Cynthia was adamant that her department was well run and that there were not many compliance issues that the district needed to fix. The state review left her with a sour taste. She found it insulting that the review used procedural compliance as a baseline for determining compliance with IDEA, because she and her staff went above and beyond to serve most families in the district.

Several other district staff members who were involved in the self-review process had a less negative reaction to the compliance review, though. One teacher told me she thought the "review was helpful in terms of reflecting on our existing systems and practices, but at the same time I don't really know what exactly the state was searching for." She expressed that she appreciated "holistically looking at student files"; however, no one I spoke to who was involved in the review process expressed that state involvement drastically changed their practices. Rather, as one staff member told me, it made her aware that the district had comprehensive IEP files, and it also "made me more aware of all the forms I need to make sure are in place." Across the board, though, the review was described as being primarily focused on procedural compliance, and nothing else.

According to Cynthia, the citation was also unfounded because Huntertown did not have many compliance issues. Cynthia and her staff often substantively applied the terms of IDEA to practice. What IDEA could offer, or did offer, was often promised to or given to students and families. And, for most students in the district, special education meetings lasted for hours and considerable resources were channeled toward students with disabilities. The minor issues of noncompliance that were found when Huntertown was first cited for disproportionality presented more of a headache to Cynthia than a push to reflect on district practices.

I realized just how trivial compliance was in relationship to the district's citation when Cynthia would ask me to make copies of a form or sheet of paper and fax it to the state. These copies and faxes were her "proof" of compliance with IDEA as each Xerox or fax represented a modification to a form, like an additional signature line or box to check off, that Cynthia made to please the state. During one of my copy-machine trips, Cynthia joked that the copies were "ridiculous." She added, "You know, it [fixing noncompliance] is like the state is telling you, 'You are in trouble and you are in time-out. Oh, and by the way, while you are on time-out make some copies and fax things to us!'" Cynthia laughed when she told me this because she saw very little purpose in the things she had to adjust to meet compliance. She was more concerned with what parents wanted from her than with what a state auditor's compliance assessment said. She was confident that she and her staff went "above and beyond" the terms of the law to serve students and families and this was evidence enough that educators in the district faithfully adhered to the intent of IDEA and provided equal educational opportunity to all students, despite the fact that the district had a history of disproportionality citations.

Toward the end of the school year, the district became 100% compliant with IDEA's mandates under Indicator 9. Cynthia had a meeting with the state representative to discuss the district's achievement. I was not at the meeting, but Cynthia told me she was angered by it. She said that the state auditor had been "very pleased" with the district and "appreciated that Huntertown was no longer providing lip service [about addressing dispro-portionality] because real changes were made in the district," as evidenced by Cynthia's ability to show full regulatory compliance with IDEA. Cynthia felt as if the state were "kudo-ing" itself in the meeting. She told me, "I am confident that me and all my staff have and do all that we can" to help the students "prior to and after the state's intervention." She found little to no connection between the state auditor's monitoring and the quality of edu-cational services she and her staff provided to students in the district. For her, procedural compliance had nothing to do with how she served students.

THE LIMITS OF THE LAW

Across all three districts, the logic of compliance shaped how educators understood and approached efforts to address disproportionality through IDEA. In Sunderville, procedural and symbolic compliance dominated edu-cational practice. In Gerrytown, the gap between the formal structures and informal norms and culture of the district diluted the positive impact IDEA could have on student outcomes. And in Huntertown, the educators in the district used their record of substantive compliance with IDEA to prove that educational opportunities were given to all students, despite several years of citations for disproportionality. Collectively, the social forces asso-ciated with the logic of compliance contributed to the production of racial-ized outcomes, because there is very little within the legislative structure of IDEA, or its associated compliance assessments, that pushes educators to think beyond the logic of compliance in order to ensure that educational and racial equity is achieved in special education. Therefore, the assumption that compliance with a civil rights law and policy like IDEA will produce equal educational outcomes must be questioned. And the logic of compli-ance should be challenged because in order to achieve equity, people must be willing to rupture existing scripts, procedures, and organizational struc-tures to truly combat racialized disparate outcomes (Haney Lopez, 2000). They cannot just comply to comply, because there are broader ideological and social forces that thwart the best intentions in people, policies, and educational practice.

In addition, while IDEA was not designed to explicitly discriminate against any group of students—in fact, it was designed to do the opposite—its application to practice has produced racialized outcomes for decades. Somehow, the civil rights gains of students with disabilities have become in-tertwined with the marginalization of students of color in special education. This outcome is symptomatic of the way in which race has been historically recognized in both public policy and law in the United States. It also exposes the limits of law to address a complex social issue like disproportionality.

Obasogie (2013), in his study on how people who are blind experience and understand race, illustrates how racial ideologies are deeply embedded in social interactions, policy, and law. He states that "social practices train individuals to look differently on certain bodies" (p. 62), regardless of a person's capacity to "see" skin color, finding that racial discrimination is not solely a reaction to visibly different skin colors, but rather is embedded in the social fabric of everyday life. Obasogie asserts that notions of race, superiority, and inferiority are deeply engrained in seemingly mundane social interactions and benign social practices that equally shape sighted and not sighted individuals' notions of race. These unspoken and unseen social understandings of race ultimately affect how policies and laws are conceptualized, created, and implemented across various social settings. However, sensitivity to this complex understanding of race, and acknowledgment of often-unseen racial ideologies in the social world, are not evident in the most well intentioned policies—and especially not in the disproportionality-monitoring mechanisms.

Obasogie (2013) also states that equal protection jurisprudence, which constitutes a foundational premise of IDEA, since the *Regents of the University of California v. Bakke* (1978)[1] decision, "has evolved in a manner that reduces race to a series of discrete categories that exist outside of any broader social or political process and whose significance and salience are thought to come from mere observation," alluding to how policy and law treat race solely as a visually identifiable trait (p. 157). In relationship to special education, the way in which race and disproportionality has been and is conceptualized in the policy prescriptions of IDEA is one-dimensional, focused on solely counting the bodies of students by their race and their disability category through numerical thresholds that are then remedied through compliance mechanisms. This policy approach means that each category—race and disability—is treated as a decontextualized numerical entity that triggers procedural remedies. The policy approach deletes the sociological complexity of how "race" operates in society and it also negates the impact that social context, material and resource inequalities, and human interactions have on the production of racialized educational inequities. More specifically, race, and in this case disproportionate outcomes, becomes a numerical category that can be "fixed" through compliance remedies that require little to no recognition of how social context and norms affect racialized inequities. This decontextualized approach is embedded in educational interventions like RtI and PBIS, and it also influences the logic of compliance.

In summary, the persistence of disproportionality in special education suggests that the civil rights intent of IDEA has not been realized in practice. It also suggests that ensuring equal opportunity through IDEA does not sufficiently challenge structures of inequality, because laws that are founded on the premise of equal treatment, or opportunity, as it is written in IDEA, allow for inequalities to be reproduced under the guise of equal treatment as equal protection (Harris, 1993). Thus, if educators are providing educational opportunities, as evidenced through compliance with IDEA, then a disparate outcome like disproportionality cannot be their fault or that of the social conditions within their school or district. Instead, this reasoning allows for unequal educational outcomes to be blamed on students and families because, under the guise of compliance, educators are not explicitly discriminating against students.

Moving Beyond the Compliance Paradigm

Bowker and Star (2000), in their work on human classification systems, analyzed how the racial classification system associated with South African apartheid justified overt and cruel discrimination, illustrating just how powerful classification and organizational systems are when they are presumed to be neutral and/or are taken for granted as "natural." Bowker and Star (2000) argue that in an organizational system that justifies something like apartheid, people who are complying with the system are just as guilty of discriminatory actions as someone who is blatantly racist. They state that "the quiet bureaucrat 'just following orders' is in a way more chilling" (p.196) than someone who is overtly racist. Bowker and Star (2000) raise an important point about the seemingly benign, yet nefarious role compliance can play when compliance means complacency with social norms and ways of being that justify racial inequities.

While Bowker and Star's (2000) analogy may seem extreme in relationship to the topic of this book, it does surface important questions about the role that we, as educators, researchers, policymakers, and the like, have in reproducing racial inequities in special education when we comply with IDEA and/or assume the legislation is racially neutral and fairly applied to practice. It also raises questions about how our everyday decisions, orientations, and interactions toward special education and disproportionality relate to persistent inequities. For instance, why is it that compliance seems to be the primary solution that the federal government, SEAs, LEAs, and educators look toward in order to address disproportionality, despite evidence of prior success in abating the issue? What are the equity implications when compliance with IDEA becomes a means to an end? Who is actually benefiting from compliance with IDEA? And, most important, what exactly are the equity implications of our everyday actions on students' lives when we comply with IDEA?

The stories that are told in this book, about well-intentioned educators trying to comply with IDEA, answer some of these questions. Through the lens of fragmentation of harm (Payne, 1984), the stories illustrate how the educators' actions produced intended and unintended disparate outcomes through chains of interactions that extended across different individuals, organizational units, and institutional boundaries that made it relatively difficult for each of them to understand the aggregate impacts of their everyday actions on inequality. And, as Payne (1984) argues, fragmentation of harm occurs even though people may be conducting their work "with the best interests of those at hand" (p. 41) and to the best of their ability. However, the decisions and choices made in the course of a day may unintentionally harm or discriminate against, deny or give opportunity to, one group or person over another. Over time, these decisions can lead to unequal outcomes, because the social context and organizational norms of schools and districts, coupled with colorblind and race-neutral approaches to education, allow for educators to treat compliance as a means to an end, rather than an opportunity to question how people, policies, procedures, and educational practices can be aligned to achieve equity in special education.

Given the social forces that influence the logic of compliance, the question still remains to be answered when pursuing educational equity: Does compliance matter in special education? The answer is not a simple one. The chapters of this book have illustrated that when, why, and how IDEA compliance matters is intimately linked to the social contexts within which it is used and the professional capacity of educators which has equity implications when addressing disproportionality in special education.

DOES COMPLIANCE MATTER IN SPECIAL EDUCATION?

Chapter 1 made it abundantly clear that compliance with IDEA matters given the historical exclusion and marginalization of students with disabilities in the U.S. education system. Through the passage of PL 94-142, the EAHCA, and IDEA, students with disabilities, who had been systematically denied the right to a free appropriate public education, slowly gained educational access and opportunity through disability legislation. However, as the legislation developed, it became procedurally dense and has negatively impacted educational practice; the social justice impetus of IDEA has been replaced with an enforcement structure that is focused on evidence of procedural compliance, not equity. This has generated an environment where educators can symbolically comply with IDEA and satisfice in a way that is responsive to their local sociocultural context. Compliance in this manner does not challenge educators' biases and beliefs and/or the social norms that influence how educational services are delivered to diverse students. These biases, beliefs, and social norms collectively thwart the legislative intent of IDEA when it is applied to practice.

Chapter 2 explored how disproportionality relates to structural and interactional opportunity gaps in varying social contexts. The chapter illustrates how broader educational opportunity gaps and/or resource inequalities, coupled with the influence of social contextual factors on educational outcomes like sociodemographic changes and/or the historical legacy of segregation and failed integration of school districts, affect how IDEA is used in educational practice. It also shows how the legislative promise of equal educational opportunity and access through IDEA is not provided equally to all students, particularly to Black and Latinx males, because of broader structural and interactional opportunity gaps. This puts in doubt that IDEA compliance alone is an effective means for addressing disproportionality. Lastly, the chapter shows that despite the best intentions of educators, compliance with IDEA cannot sufficiently counter the complex historical and social forces that influence how educational opportunities and resources are given to students across and within schools.

In Chapter 3, the relationship between educational leaders, disproportionality, and IDEA compliance was explored for its equity implications. The chapter shows how the organizational, sociodemographic, cultural context, professional capacities, and norms of a school district influence how leaders approach their work. It also indicates that educational leaders must be intentional in their pursuit of educational equity, because if they are not, their unexamined micro-actions, in the aggregate, lead to disparate outcomes, and educational inequities are, intentionally or not, reproduced on a daily basis. In addition, because the sources of disproportionality are extremely complex, educational leaders must be systematic and intentional in pursuing equity because local norms and ways of being can dislodge the best intentions in people, policies, and practices. Lastly, the chapter indicates that leaders must resist the inertia of the status quo and push their staff and organizational systems to align around achieving equity, not just compliance, because compliance alone is insufficient for addressing racial inequities.

Chapter 4 illustrated that compliance in special education really matters *if* parents and/or guardians can leverage it to benefit their own children. The chapter shows how parents are the main drivers of IDEA enforcement. If parents and/or guardians have strong social networks and connections with school officials and if they are welcomed to substantively participate in educational decisionmaking processes, they can leverage the power granted to them through IDEA to make use of opportunity hoarding to benefit their children. However, this individualistic approach to securing educational opportunity and access via IDEA is fraught with equity implications. The educational system differentially rewards and responds to varying habitus, means of parental engagement, and social and cultural capital. And schools have historically validated the social and cultural practices of dominant cultures through colorblind and race-neutral frameworks. Collectively, these factors ensure that the distribution of educational services and interventions to *all* students via IDEA will most likely be unequal and inequitable if parents and/or guardians remain the primary enforcers of IDEA legislation.

Lastly, the logic of compliance was outlined in Chapter 5. The chapter provides the analytical tools needed to understand how IDEA's civil rights intent, procedural compliance, and social and cultural contexts of schools and districts relate to disproportionality in special education. The chapter shows that compliance does matter because, whether or not compliance is effective in addressing disproportionality, educators have to comply in order to remain professionally legitimate. However, while the logic of compliance allows for districts, schools, and educators to continue to do their work in a socially acceptable manner, compliance distances educators from the students they must serve. This is because IDEA and the disproportionality monitoring mechanisms within it do not account for how often unseen racial ideologies in the social world influence policies, procedures, and everyday educational practices, which contribute to the production of racial inequities in special education. The chapter essentially outlines the paradox and dilemma associated with the need to comply with IDEA and the reality that compliance often contributes to inequities in special education. Therefore, when pursuing educational equity, the question arises again: Does compliance matter in special education? This book show that yes, it does matter, but in unexpected and complicated ways.

THE BOUNDARIES OF THE COMPLIANCE PARADIGM

The seemingly inescapable compliance paradigm that engulfs special education in the United States is a complex problem that is shaped by the logic of compliance. It constrains how educators can respond to students and families when providing educational services. It is also deeply embedded in the professional culture and norms of everyday educational practice. The compliance paradigm has created an iron cage of bureaucracy that stifles creative solutions to complex equity problems.

The educational professionals working within Huntertown, Gerrytown, and Sunderville, and more broadly within SEAs and LEAs across the United States, must comply with IDEA even if it makes their work harder or seems contraindicative to their professional instincts, as shirking compliance is both legally and morally wrong. And, complicating the matter, if the educational professionals in this book did not comply with IDEA, they would be subject to additional state audits and potential federal sanctions; noncompliance is not a viable option. Lastly, 100% compliance with IDEA, was and is the end goal for the three districts, and for districts across the United States, because noncompliance implies that an SEA, LEA, school, and/or educational professional is discriminating against students with disabilities and not committed to providing equal educational opportunity and FAPE. This is an indictment that few, if any, educational professionals want to be implicated in. However, when educators rely upon the logic of compliance to address a complex issue like disproportionality, their actions actually contribute to the production of racialized outcomes in special education. This is not solely related to the individual capacities of educators, though; rather, it is intimately tied to the fact that schools and districts across the United States are engulfed within a compliance paradigm that does not provide space for educators to sufficiently consider the effects that social context and their own personal and professional capacities and beliefs have on their educational practice when using educational policy. This limits how educators are able to systematically and thoughtfully address inequities in special education, which ultimately negatively affects students.

Neo-institutional theorists DiMaggio and Powell (1983) posit that organizational and professional fields create an "iron cage" around social actors that constrains how they can respond to and react to their environments. This iron cage is maintained through organizational constraints that are sustained by three isomorphic social forces: mimetic, normative, and coercive (DiMaggio & Powell, 1983).[1] Isomorphism is the process whereby organizations within a particular organizational field, often embedded in vastly different social contexts and circumstances, like school districts across the United States, tend to look and act similarly when addressing complex issues as they face similar constraints and environmental conditions. They do this despite evidence of prior success in addressing the complex issue. Mimetic isomorphic forces are characterized by individuals looking to others in similar situations for guidance on how to address multifaceted and complex problems; this perpetuates homogeneity in organizational responses to complex problems. Coercive isomorphic forces are characterized by culturally accepted rules of action in a particular field or job. These include regulatory, legal, and policy pressures that shape organizational environments and the political need to comply with them. Normative forces are influenced by the professional norms of an organizational field and shape how an individual acts and understands his or her work.

Isomorphism relates to disproportionality because schools across the United States face similar procedural and legislative constraints associated with IDEA. They must comply with the complex legislation when cited for disproportionality, a form of coercive isomorphism, even though compliance does not mean that disproportionality is actually abated (e.g., Albrecht et al., 2012; Cavendish, Artiles, & Harry, 2014; U.S. Government Accountability Office [GAO], 2013). Contributing to the iron cage of compliance is the fact that SEAs and LEAs tend to look to each other for models on how to address the issue, a form of mimetic isomorphism. Many states have similar processes for conducting state audits and the associated compliance assessments when an LEA is cited for disproportionality. This is done despite evidence of their effectiveness in addressing disproportionality. In addition, SEAs and LEAs have to focus on compliance and compliance assessments because it is an expected norm in their field, a form of normative isomorphism. These isomorphic pressures tend to constrain individuals' actions and limit their potential to generate creative solutions existing outside of the compliance paradigm to address complex equity issues. This has major equity implications, because when people uncritically comply with and adhere to the norms and rules of a professional field that has produced racialized outcomes for decades, they are inadvertently complicit in reproducing an inequity like disproportionality.

I saw clearly the negative effects of the compliance paradigm in action when I attended a district collaborative meeting with Cynthia during fieldwork. During this visit I witnessed how deeply entangled the educators were in the compliance paradigm and in isomorphic pressures. I also saw how the logic of compliance extended far beyond just the three districts included in this study.

The District Collaborative

Every few months, Roger, Cynthia, and Marc had to attend a "District Collaborative" meeting. These meetings were held in various places near their districts. They usually consisted of approximately 30 district administrators coming together in a centralized location so that they could discuss special education trends, concerns, and issues affecting students with disabilities within their region. The meetings also served as a space and place for the administrators to pool their resources and discuss private school placements, the availability of more restrictive environments within the region, and how they could build their capacity to provide more intense intervention services for students with severe needs.

In the late spring I attended a District Collaborative meeting with Cynthia. It was held in a small building that felt dark and cramped. The building had one bathroom and one large room with windows that looked out on a nearby highway. It was a nondescript and simple place. All of the administrators in the large room sat around a huge table in a semicircle, which ensured that the administrators got a clear view of the cars passing by on the busy highway only a few feet away from the building.

Cynthia and I were about 10 minutes late to the meeting because of traffic. And she told me she wasn't particularly fond of District Collaborative meetings, so she was not in a rush to get there. After we arrived, we settled into the back of the room while the leader of the District Collaborative, Mrs. Frantanelli, spoke about Medicaid.

Mrs. Frantanelli appeared to be frustrated as she spoke about a form that all the district administrators had to make sure was completed in order for the districts to receive their Medicaid funds. As she spoke about the form an administrator raised his hand and asked Mrs. Frantanelli why they (the administrators in the room) were responsible for filling out this new form when they already have district-specific Medicaid forms. Mrs. Frantanelli replied with, "because this is the office of redundancy office," implying that regardless of what the districts already did, she needed another form completed by the administrators so that she could send it to "state ed." She was clearly frustrated by this fact, but quickly asked the administrators if they understood what they needed to do, and then moved on to the next agenda item.

I soon realized that this was Mrs. Frantanelli's modus operandi in the meeting. She would present a topic, field a few questions, express her thoughts on the issue, and then move on. She dominated the meeting with a rapid pace and ran through multiple agenda items in a short period of time. I also realized that many of the agenda items she slated for the meeting were approached in a somewhat technical manner that focused on streamlining compliance measures across all of the districts rather than talking about substantive issues in practice.

The next agenda item that she brought up was related to an RtI initiative, a procedural mandate, and parental consent. Mrs. Frantanelli asked the group if they were OK if the District Collaborative reached out to parents regarding the procedural mandate so she could "streamline the paperwork and compliance processes surrounding the initiative." The question prompted an administrator to raise her hand and say, "I cannot believe the layers of paperwork now," referring to the burden of compliance mandates, and added, "I am more than happy to have the collaborative take over a layer of reporting to the state because it is less I have to do with the paperwork!" The room reverberated with a muted chatter and most of the administrators informally commented that they liked the idea. With this, Mrs. Frantanelli then stated, "OK, the collaborative will do it," and then she moved on to the next agenda item, entitled "ESL."

As Mrs. Frantanelli started to talk about the "ESL" agenda item, I could tell something was different in her approach toward this topic. She appeared to be both agitated and desperate to get the administrators to listen to her empathetically as she spoke. I noticed this because as she embarked on the agenda item, she sat up straighter in her chair and pulled her chair closer to the table. She specifically mentioned several times that she wanted to evaluate "the benefit of [giving] services [ESL] to kids with an IQ of, say, 40." The students she was talking about were those who have serious cognitive delays and who are legally mandated to receive both special education and ESL services.

Mrs. Frantanelli spoke at length about how "state ed" had convened a committee to discuss how special education and ESL mandates intersect, because the need to deliver both services to students was "burdening" educators. She stated:

> I think some of the ESL regulations are contraindicative to
> the needs of special education students . . . again, I am talking

about kids with an IQ, say, of 40. I find it ludicrous to pull out
a kid from their appropriate [special education] environment
because of an ESL mandate. The notion of pulling out a kid
for ESL instruction with an IQ of 40?!?! To what end, exactly?
To be with a teacher that is not trained to address their
disabilities, but can provide ESL services? What's the point?

Mrs. Frantanelli was frustrated because giving ESL services to students
with low cognitive skills did not make sense to her. She told the group that
she has shared her thoughts with "state ed" numerous times and found it
"ludicrous" that "no solutions" had been proposed to seriously address the
issue.

After delivering these statements, Mrs. Frantanelli looked at the group
and said, "If you don't offer it [ESL services], then you are stuck with an
impartial hearing and legal ramifications if you don't provide 2 hours of
[ESL] pullout!" She outlined how high the stakes were if the administrators did not comply with the intersecting mandates. She added, "I have no
problem not providing the 2 hours of pullout," but "you may feel differently because you have to face the legal ramifications." With this statement,
Cynthia nudged me and whispered, "Of course she doesn't care because the
state won't be on her. We are the ones that have to pay," alluding to the fact
that the districts would have to deal with impartial hearings, state auditors,
and the ramifications of being noncompliant with IDEA and ESL mandates.

The group was quiet as Mrs. Frantanelli spoke, which seemed to prompt
her to continue. She told the administrators, "I cannot handle you paying
an exorbitant fee to provide ESL services for very low-level kids," adding,
"however, of course you [the directors] should offer the services to more
able students so you [the districts] do not expose yourselves to corrective
action." As she spoke, she appeared to be walking a fine line between compliance, noncompliance, and outright denial of educational services to students whose lives merged at the intersection between a disability label and
English as a Second Language label. She also seemed to be trying to resolve
the tension between the burden of managing multiple mandates and the
need to comply with the impact that these mandates had on the educators
in the room and on educational practice.

Mrs. Frantanelli continued to be the only one speaking until she began
to talk about the economic costs of providing both ESL and special education services to low-functioning students. She said, "We are in an economic
time where we are literally looking at pennies" when servicing students with
disabilities. This comment finally prompted an administrator to speak out.
The administrator raised her hand and said quietly, "We are struggling with
this." Her comment started a collective chatter in the room that lasted for
several minutes.

Mrs. Frantanelli finally broke the chatter by stating, "I don't understand why on earth you would pull out a self-contained kid for 2 hours to a non-special-education–trained ESL teacher," adding that this practice does not help students and that it is again "contraindicative" to the needs of students with disabilities. She finished with a booming, "It's insane!" With this last comment, Mrs. Frantanelli asked the directors, "Would you like us to provide these services for very impaired kids or would you like to not [provide the services], knowing that if audited you will go to corrective action?"

Her question raised a profound tension between the need to comply and the mimetic, normative, and coercive forces that were affecting all of the administrators in the room. They were trapped within the compliance paradigm: They had to comply; they were professionally trained to comply and provide interventions through IDEA; and they felt normative and professional pressures from multiple sources to comply. But compliance made their work very hard to do and it didn't seem to serve students well, either. And although the administrators in the room had very different social contexts within which they worked, they were immersed in an organizational field that demanded compliance at any cost, which, whether intended or not, inadvertently denied educational opportunity to some of their students.

Mrs. Frantanelli's question about not complying spurred many of the administrators in the room to speak up. One administrator said, "We really need mandate relief for this because it doesn't make sense." Another administrator, who was sitting next to Mrs. Frantanelli, shared his story about how he dealt with the "ESL issue." The administrator told the group that he sat down with a state representative to handle the "ESL issue" and created a form that parents could sign that acknowledged that they consented to their child not receiving ESL services. The administrator said that despite the fact that he created the parental consent form with a state representative, when his district was audited by the state he was cited for being noncompliant with the "ESL issue." Mrs. Frantanelli interjected at this point and said, "The state said that their form was OK, then they told us it was not!" She added with apparent frustration, "Maybe someone should check on how the state is doing things!"

Another administrator used the flow of conversation to speak up. She stated, "You know, it is hard because there are no ESL parents championing their [ESL students'] rights like there are with disability parents." This comment was the first time that I heard someone speak about civil rights concerns—an hour and a half into the meeting—and question how educational opportunities were provided to students who were classified both as having a disability and needing language services. The same administrator finished her statement with, "I do think it is wrong to have them [the students] go to ESL and not get the required mandated special education services they need." This prompted another administrator to say that because of the "ESL issue," they have actually "put all ESL kids in one school" so they can streamline services. Essentially, the administrator programmatically segregated students so that it was easier for her to give the "ESL kids" their mandated services. This is in direct contrast to the spirit of IDEA, which is focused on inclusion, rather than seclusion, but it was in line with the need to comply with IDEA at any cost. After this last comment, Mrs. Frantanelli pivoted the conversation to the next agenda item. But before she completely abandoned the "ESL issue," she added that she wanted to hear about how "everyone is dealing with this as time passes."

The depth and reach of the compliance paradigm was immense. The educators attending the District Collaborative struggled to meet the procedural mandates and paperwork demands of IDEA, they struggled to avoid state audits of their educational practices, and they struggled to meet the needs of students labeled at the intersection between language acquisition and disability. The convergence between the compliance paradigm and the ESL mandates put severe pressure on the administrators to comply at any cost, despite their best intentions. And when the administrators followed the professional norms and expectations of their field, they unintentionally allowed for educational opportunity gaps to manifest and persist for vulnerable students.

In summary, the experiences of the administrators in this ethnographic moment make it abundantly clear that efforts to address complex educational issues must move beyond a compliance paradigm. This is difficult though, because the U.S. special education system is supported by an immense bureaucratic structure and professional culture that prioritizes procedural compliance with IDEA in order to achieve equality and equity in education. Instead of focusing on compliance, people working in the field must be willing to disrupt the status quo, challenge everyday acts of compliance, and question how the procedures, policies, everyday routines, and organizational structures that surround the delivery of special education services in schools may actually contribute to, rather than ameliorate, inequities and disproportionate outcomes in special education.

CHALLENGING THE COMPLIANCE PARADIGM

What is necessary, then, to challenge the hidden inequities of practice associated with compliance with IDEA? For one, educational leaders, educators, and other educational stakeholders must embrace the tensions that arise from challenging taken-for-granted social systems and ways of being that reproduce inequities. They cannot simply comply with them. This requires that educators identify the contours of their local "zone(s) of mediation" (Welner, 2001) and push the boundaries of this zone.

The zone of mediation is comprised of broad cultural norms, ways of being, and "power relations and values" that "set the parameters of beliefs, behavior and policy in schools" (Welner, 2001, p. 96). Holme at al. (2014), borrowing from Oakes et al., (2005), elaborate upon the concept and explain how school districts act as "mediating institutions" of broader social, political, and economic forces that shape the zone of mediation. Holme et al. (2014) state, "viewing schools as mediating institutions can help to better explain why the adoption and implementation of reforms that seek to improve outcomes for traditionally marginalized populations can be so difficult, because such reforms often run up against existing dynamics of power" (p. 40). These dynamics of power are associated with the four dimensions of the zone of mediation that must be challenged in the pursuit of educational equity.

The four dimensions of the zone of mediation include inertial, technical, normative, and political forces (Welner, 2001). The normative and political dimensions take on a greater significance when equity-minded reform is initiated because they require that political, material, and ideological turfs are actively contested within local contexts (Welner, 2001). Therefore, in order to address deep-seated and systemic special education inequities like disproportionality, educators should actively engage with and challenge their local zones of mediation (Welner, 2001) and initiate third-order change (Renee, Welner & Oakes, 2010; Welner, 2001).

Third-order change requires that fundamental shifts are made to "educators' and community members' core normative beliefs about such matters as race, class, intelligence and educability" (Welner, 2001, p. 239) in their pursuit of educational equity. Third-order change cannot be accomplished or initiated, though, when an individualized compliance paradigm is relied upon that is fundamentally detached from the complexities of everyday educational practice. Therefore, when educational stakeholders are able to understand the social forces that shape their local zone(s) of mediation they can push the boundaries of the zone(s) and challenge the compliance paradigm. This requires that educators identify how their own belief systems, their staff members' belief systems, and the policies and practices operating in their local context both constrain equity-minded reform efforts and provide opportunities for meaningful change. If educators are willing to do this, third-order change (Renee, Welner, & Oakes, 2010; Welner, 2001) is possible.

Inertial Forces

Inertial forces are the taken-for-granted ways of being in an institution. These are the unquestioned habits, routines, and practices that exist in organizations that self-perpetuate without much effort (Welner, 2001). They are powerful and they shape how educators relate to their students and ultimately affect how they enact educational policies, procedures, and practices. This is because inertial forces are tied to local ways of being that are taken for granted as "normal," implying that inertial forces are often unseen and that people enact them without realizing the equity implications of their actions on student outcomes.

In relation to this point, Mendoza, Paguyo, and Gutierrez (2015) state, in their analysis on the intersections of race, culture, and disability, that "common sense," or taken-for-granted ways of being are "so grounded in social practices and dominant ideologies that good intentions alone are not a guarantee that equity work will be done" (p. 77). It is this realization about inertial social forces—that good intentions in policies, people, procedures, and practices are insufficient for addressing disproportionality—that must be recognized by all educators and must spur them to work intentionally to address educational inequities, rather than comply because they must comply.

In a similar vein, critical legal scholar Ian Haney Lopez (2000) states that racialized disparities will continue to persist in many realms of American society because people only have to "show up" and comply with the systems that already exist in order to ensure that systems of inequity and racial inequities perpetuate (p. 1757). In this legal critique, Haney Lopez (2000) decenters the assumption that law and policy, as they are currently designed, are effective in combatting racialized outcomes. Therefore, when we just "show up" to work, as Haney Lopez states, and comply with the systems before us, we are by default responsible for whatever outcomes result from our acts of complicit compliance, and our unquestioned participation with inertial forces actually contributes to the production of racial inequities.

The impact of inertial forces on disproportionality can be seen throughout the pages of this book and within the logic of compliance and the compliance paradigm. The inertia surrounding the assumption that compliance with IDEA is effective in addressing student needs does not sufficiently account for the professional capacities and beliefs of educators and organizational, social, and policy pressures that subvert the best intentions of people, policies, and practices. It also does not engage with racial ideologies and the social and contextual factors that negatively impact student outcomes and marginalize families.

Some concrete steps that can be taken to challenge inertial forces within districts and schools include, but are not limited to, these actions:

- Ensuring that district and school offices are warm and welcoming to *all* students, families, and community partners;
- Ensuring that *all* families and student voices are meaningfully integrated into school- and districtwide operations;
- Ensuring that there is awareness among district- and school-based

staff that there are ideological and taken-for-granted cultural
norms in the schooling process that advantage some students over
others;

- Ensuring that staff know that curricula should be critically
interrogated for the accurate representation of all groups of
students and that curricula sufficiently acknowledge structures of
power and privilege in society;
- Ensuring that there is community-wide knowledge of racial
inequities and disproportionality occurring in the district via
regular school and district communication channels; and
- Ensuring that educational inequities are clearly described in
district communications so that community and school coalitions
can be formed to address the inequities.

These suggestions are loosely adapted from Bryk et al. (2010); Fergus
(2016); and Klingner et al. (2005).

Technical Forces

The technical forces associated with the zone of mediation are the tangible,
material, and temporal inputs of an organization that give it structure, and
influence resource allocations within schools (Welner, 2001). These can include funding formulas, school district zoning laws, educators' preparation
programs, student schedules, and the like. Technical forces are often related
to policymakers and educational leaders because their decisions often have
systemwide impacts. These forces are the most concrete inputs related to the
zone of mediation because they are often visible and the inputs associated
with technical forces can be physically manipulated.

In terms of special education and disproportionality, national- and
state-level funding formulas associated with IDEA implementation should
be critically examined for their impact on patterns of racial disproportionality in classification, placement, and suspension (e.g., Parrish, 2002). In addition, the ways in which educational leaders allocate resources, both material
and professional, across districts and within schools have to be critically
examined for their equity impacts on diverse students (e.g., Parrish, 2002;
Parrish & Wolman, 2004). This requires that district- and school-based administrators not only meet their budgetary needs, but that they do so in a
way that is consistently cognizant of the equity impacts of their decisions on
historically marginalized students. They also need to be aware of how local
contextual conditions, like segregation and failed integration, affect how
they can allocate resources so that they can challenge inequitable policies
and practices. Thus, educators and leaders must have both technical and
critical knowledge of the boundaries that shape their workflow so that they
can challenge the zone mediation.

In addition, educational leaders need to be better prepared to deal with the technical complexities of special education law so that they are knowledgeable about special education regulations and are thus able to find ways to challenge the compliance paradigm. Problematically though, Pazey and Cole (2013), in their review of literature on special education leadership preparation programs, find that administrators are unprepared to navigate the "complex maze of legal requirements" that are related to special education law and other educational accountability laws (p. 246). Pazey and Cole (2013) advocate that special education and special education law courses be added to *all* educational leadership programs across the United States. They raise an important point, because if educational leaders do not have sufficient knowledge of the laws and policies that shape the administration of special education services in schools and districts, they cannot, arguably, fully identify their zone of mediation and challenge the compliance paradigm.

Some concrete steps that can be taken to ensure that technical forces are challenged in the zone of mediation include, but are not limited to, these actions:

- Ensuring that funding, space, and time are regularly allocated for districtwide *collaborative* professional development related to issues of race, disability, ethnicity, equity, inclusion, diversity, sexuality, country of origin, and so forth;
- Ensuring that within-school tracking is monitored for racial, ethnic, linguistic, and gender patterns;
- Ensuring that a schoolwide equity plan and mission statement is established and abided by, that guides students' schedules and the allocation of experienced teachers to high-needs classrooms;
- Ensuring that efforts to address inequities and disproportionality are integrated into all strategic decisions and that resource allocations are targeted toward addressing known inequities in a school or district;
- Ensuring that district- and schoolwide policies are established that proactively and regularly examine disaggregated student achievement, behavior, and attendance data by race, ethnicity, gender, gifted-and-talented status, and so forth;
- Ensuring that the most qualified teachers are assigned to the highest-need classes and that there is diversity in the teaching force; and
- Ensuring that local social service and community-based organizations are involved with district and school operations in order to strategically align the resources needed to support equity in educational outcomes.

These suggestions are loosely adapted from Bryk et al. (2010), Fergus (2016), and Klingner et al. (2005).

Normative Forces

Normative forces shape how educators approach their work and include personal and professional beliefs and values (Welner, 2001). Normative forces are also deeply entrenched within local communities and within broader ideologies that define such things as achievement, race, and teacher expectations. These social forces are very strong and are very difficult to challenge because they are associated with a person's core belief system (Welner, 2001). However, one way in which educators and educational leaders can think concretely about challenging normative forces is by learning from the findings of Pollock, Deckman, Mira, and Shalaby's (2010) study on a preservice teacher preparation program focused on racial justice.

Pollock et al. (2010) found that when the preservice educators in their sample were asked to think about the role of race and inequities in their own educational practice, they encountered personal, structural, and strategic tensions that resulted in the educators asking themselves the question "*What can I do?*" across all three tensions. At the personal level, the authors found that the study's participants questioned their own readiness to engage with and talk about issues related to race and racism. At the structural level, the participants struggled to understand how they could combat racial inequities and social injustices via the classroom. And, at the strategic level, the participants searched for concrete socially conscious strategies and actions that they could implement in their classroom on a daily basis. Across all three tensions, the educators questioned their own efficacy and capacity to positively effect socially just outcomes via their classrooms. The authors suggest that educators should engage with these three tensions throughout their educational practice because they are necessary reflections in the pursuit for racially and socially just educational outcomes.

Pollock et al.'s (2010) findings provide a roadmap for the mindsets that are needed to challenge normative social forces because educators, leaders, and educational stakeholders must constantly remain reflective about the roles that race, racism, and educational inequalities play in disparate educational outcomes. In addition, Pollock et al.'s (2010) framework pushes educators to reflect upon how equity work relates to their personal lives and to their professional practice. It also requires educators to remain critical about how their personal and professional orientations intersect with social justice work.

In addition, it is imperative that educators actively challenge the compliance paradigm and deficit-based normative belief systems through professional development opportunities that increase cultural awareness and address personal biases related to race and class differences. This work should be focused on using something like a racially literate (Guinier & Torres, 2002), culturally sustaining (Paris & Alim, 2014, 2017), and/or culturally responsive (Gay, 2010; Ladson-Billings, 1995a, 1995b) perspective. Racial literacy sees race as relevant to all aspects of social life and constantly interrogates the dynamic relationships among race, class, geography, gender, and other explanatory variables that contribute to racialized outcomes (Guinier & Torres, 2003). Culturally sustaining pedagogy rejects cultural assimilation and the myths and stereotypes that are deeply engrained in the assimilationist culture of schools (Paris & Alim, 2017). It also recognizes that culture is fluid and teachers need to be receptive to multiple cultures in order to serve *all* students. Culturally responsive practices require educators to develop a nuanced, reflective, and critical consciousness about how race, power, and privilege operate in society (e.g., Ladson-Billings, 2001).

Some of these frameworks have been invoked in theoretical pieces focused on addressing disproportionality and/or inequities in special education. For instance, Klingner et al. (2005) theorized that a culturally responsive educational systems approach, which critically assesses the intersections between policies, practices, and people as they deliver educational services to students, can potentially address the multiple factors associated with disproportionate outcomes in special education. This approach recognizes that the intersections between policies, practices, and people can both generate disparate outcomes and provide spaces where possible solutions can be identified to address the issue. In another theoretical piece, Waitoller and Thorius (2016) connected inclusive approaches to serving students with special needs, specifically Universal Design for Learning, to the theoretical tenets of culturally sustaining pedagogy. They suggest that if the two approaches are considered together, they can improve learning conditions for *all* students. Whatever the approach taken, the theoretical pieces can serve as conceptual frameworks that inform technical assistance and professional development initiatives that are focused on addressing issues like disproportionality.

In other cases, these frameworks have actually been applied to practice in attempts to address disproportionality in special education. For example, Kozleski and Zion (2006) took a culturally relevant perspective and created a systemic assessment of policies and practices related to special education disproportionality that could be utilized by multiple stakeholder teams at the district level to address the issue. Thorius and Tan (2015) describe how this framework was refined and used by a regional equity assistance center, in collaboration with a state education department, to eliminate special education disproportionality. In addition, Bal and colleagues (Bal, Kozleski, Schrader, Rodriguez, & Pelton, 2014; Bal, Thorius, & Kozleski, 2012) have applied formative intervention (Engestrom, 2011) and, more broadly, Cultural Historical Activity Theory (CHAT) (Foot, 2001; Gutierrez, 2008;

Gutierrez, Larson, Enciso, & Ryan, 2007) to create learning laboratory methodology within local enactments of PBIS to address disproportionality. Broadly speaking, the goals of these studies are to generate points of praxis for educators to facilitate systems change and address disproportionality in discipline and/or classification and placement. Efforts like these must continue to be developed in order to disrupt and eliminate disproportionate outcomes in special education.

Some additional concrete steps that can be taken to challenge the normative forces associated with local zones of mediation include, but are not limited to these actions:

- Ensuring that educators acknowledge that professional development is a lifelong learning process;
- Ensuring that educators develop the capacity to have meaningful conversations with one another about how race, culture, diversity, equity, inclusion, sexuality, country of origin, and so forth relate to their educational practice and student outcomes;
- Ensuring that staff are aware that culture is dynamic, complex, constantly evolving, and embedded in every aspect of the teaching and learning process;
- Ensuring that student perspectives are meaningfully included in the teaching and learning process and that deficit-based beliefs about students and families are not tolerated;
- Ensuring that all school-based teams, special education offices, related service providers, educational professionals, and so forth, have a comprehensive understanding of disproportionality, and educational inequity more broadly, within their schools; and
- Ensuring that staff members are aware that they are both part of the problem and part of the solution when addressing racialized inequities in practice.

These suggestions are loosely adapted from Bryk et al. (2010); Fergus (2016); Klingner et al. (2005); Kramarczuk Voulgarides, Fergus, and Thorius (2017).

Political Forces

Lastly, the political forces that are associated with local zones of mediation are related to the power imbalances that exist within a community and that extend beyond the four walls of a school or the boundaries of a district. Political forces include the influence of local, state, and federal demands; expectations; and needs on schools (Welner, 2001). Political forces also include the power struggles that can emerge when there is a redistribution of material resources within local contexts (Oakes, Quartz, Gong, Guiton, & Lipton, 1993). Essentially, political forces include the intersection between policy mandates and economic and social power dynamics in national and local contexts, which in turn affect efforts to address educational inequities like disproportionality.

As seen in this book, it was rare for anyone from the state level, to the district level, to the school building level to challenge the political forces that were related to disproportionality and IDEA compliance because, frankly, they didn't have to. This is because the legislative structure of IDEA does not require that educators use the legislation to pursue equity; rather, it is focused on individualized remedies and technical decontextualized compliance mechanisms. Essentially, the educators did not have to challenge political forces and their zone of mediation, and state auditors did not ask them to, because compliance with IDEA—no matter how the educators used it and no matter the effects of compliance on practice—was evidence enough that disproportionality was being sufficiently addressed. Across all three districts, racial and class undertones affected how educational resources were distributed to diverse students. However, the way that the educators in each district used IDEA and complied with IDEA did not disturb the power dynamics in the districts. The educators could, and did, comply with IDEA in a way that maintained the status quo, or in other words, did not challenge locally occurring systems of inequity. Given that educational inequities are rarely challenged when people just "show up" (Haney Lopez, 2000, p. 1757) or uncritically comply with a policy like IDEA, it is important that when state-level officials and educators in LEAs interact, they operate with the recognition that the logic of compliance and the compliance paradigm can subvert their best intentions, dehumanize the impact of their work on educational practice, and ultimately harm historically marginalized students. This requires that SEA and LEA officials meaningfully collaborate and purposefully resist neoliberal and colorblind solutions to address complex equity problems like disproportionality. State officials and local educators need to find dynamic and productive ways to proactively engage with and challenge the complex political forces that surround issues of educational equity within local contexts.

 For example, state auditors should not solely demand evidence of compliance with IDEA mandates from LEAs when addressing disproportionality and LEA officials should not allow evidence of compliance alone to be the primary mechanism for addressing locally occurring inequities. State auditors and officials should recognize the impact that local demographic factors and a history of segregation and/or failed integration have on an educator's capacity to use IDEA to benefit all students within local contexts and use this knowledge, in conjunction with LEA representatives, to push local zones of mediation. Educators within LEAs should also be reflective of how educational resources are locally distributed and be ready to address the equity impacts associated with the unequal distribution of material resources within local contexts. Critical reflections like these, by both SEA and

LEA officials, need to be embedded into the compliance assessment process. This implies that both SEA and LEA representatives should attend collaborative and/or joint professional development initiatives that are focused on understanding how the complex sources of racial inequities intersect with and influence how IDEA is used to support students with disabilities. Collaboration of this sort requires that one party not be seen as an expert in the compliance assessment process.

Looking beyond the local level, national policy conversations about the impacts of disproportionality on student outcomes must regularly occur because the inequity has persisted despite over 20 years of federal monitoring of the issue. The Obama administration addressed some of the limitations associated with disproportionality monitoring when, in December 2016, the U.S. Department of Education announced regulatory changes to IDEA. The changes "establish a standard approach that States must use in determining whether or not significant disproportionality based on race or ethnicity is occurring in the state and in its districts" in direct response to the Government Accountability Office (GAO) 2013 report on differential disproportionality monitoring across the United States.[2] The proposed regulations require that states use a standardized process for determining if there is numerical evidence of racial disproportionality in special education, and if states are found to have "significant disproportionality" in classification, placement, and/or discipline, they must use 15% of their federal special education monies on coordinated early-intervening services (CEIS) for special education and/or general education students. The proposed regulations also further define discipline disproportionality, and how IDEA funds can be used, and require that LEAs identify the "root causes" of inequities in policies, practices, and procedures related to the administration of special education services.[3]

While the proposed changes are a step in the right direction toward solving disproportionality in special education, they continue to rely on a compliance paradigm that may not sufficiently address the complex factors that contribute to disproportionality in special education. For example, although the development of a standardized measure for determining whether or not significant disproportionality is present in an LEA is critical for monitoring the issue, it is still fraught with unintended consequences that may push educators to focus on the number of students classified, placed, and/or disciplined, rather than on the social conditions that have led to disproportionate outcomes. This underscores how efforts to address the issue must be systemic, coordinated, purposeful, and substantively focused on both qualitative and quantitative indicators of equity that move beyond compliance assessments of policies and procedures.

The final rollout of the proposed regulations was set to begin in the 2018–2019 school year and be completed by 2020. However, the U.S. Department of Education under the Trump administration has decided to delay the proposed regulations.[4] This was done despite public resistance from civil rights groups and prominent social justice, educational, and civil rights organizations.[5]

Given the shifting political context surrounding educational policy in the United States and the difficulty associated with addressing political forces at the local level, some concrete steps that can be taken to challenge the zone of mediation at the political level include, but are not limited to, these actions:

- Ensuring that there is continued public and governmental support to establish a standardized national measure for determining significant disproportionality and that the conversation around this standardized measure includes recognition of the impacts of the compliance paradigm on educational practice;
- Ensuring that frequent and accessible communication channels (e.g., multiple languages) are formalized between state-, district-, and school-level offices and parents and/or guardians so that they, and other community stakeholders, can influence how educational policies are created and used in schools and districts;
- Ensuring that issues of equity are raised in personal and public forums between school and district officials and community and family members;
- Ensuring that LEAs regularly communicate with local and state educational officials about issues of equity occurring in their local context and discuss how state officials can help them address these issues;
- Ensuring that there is continuous local and national dialogue among policymakers and educators about how complex dynamics of power, privilege, and racial ideologies intersect with policy mandates which, in turn, affect how policies are used and how students are supported in schools; and
- Ensuring that coalitions are built between educators and community members that effectively allow for LEAs' and community members' needs to be communicated to state officials in the pursuit of educational equity.

WHAT IS THE ANSWER TO THE QUESTION?

In conclusion, disproportionality is a complex problem that is related to social, historical, political, and economic factors and to educator's beliefs and their professional capacities to solve complex equity issues. Given this, disproportionality cannot be solved solely through the individualized educational interventions and/or policy prescriptions found in IDEA legislation. And although IDEA is a civil rights law based on the 14th Amendment, which assures equal protection, and it has proven to be effective in increasing educational opportunity for historically marginalized students, its application to educational practice has not been successful in remedying racially disproportionate outcomes in the classification, placement, and/or discipline of students with disabilities.

Critical legal scholars have argued that laws founded on the premise of equal treatment, through the 14th Amendment and the equal protection clause, allow for inequalities to be reproduced under the guise of equal treatment as equal protection (Harris, 2000). Critical legal scholars have also highlighted how legal violations of the 14th Amendment can only be proven with evidence of an explicit intent to discriminate (Delgado, 1990; Harris, 2000). Skiba and colleagues (2009), in their legal analysis of Black student discipline disparities in schools, highlight the complexities associated with Equal Protection logics and the need to prove an explicit intent to discriminate when addressing discipline inequities:

> Government actions not intended to be racial in nature may have a discriminatory effect on members of certain racial or ethnic groups, including Blacks. Yet the individuals whose interest is harmed by actions motivated by non-racial concerns are not viewed as victims of racial discrimination, since it is not the consequences of government's actions that determine racial discrimination, but the intent that motivated the actions. That is, government actions are presumed to be colorblind unless it can be shown that there was an intent to discriminate based on race. (p.1105)

The quote describes a form of "colorblind constitutionalism" (Skiba et al., 2009), that limits how racial disparities in disciplinary outcomes can be remedied through federal law and policy. The problems associated with equal protection logics and colorblind constitutionalism are related to IDEA and efforts to address disproportionality for several reasons.

First, the colorblind and race neutral remedies and interventions found within IDEA minimize the significance of race on educational outcomes and they also do not sufficiently engage with the social, historical, political, and economic forces that shape how education is locally delivered and which affect racially disproportionate outcomes. Second, although both race and disability are protected classes under the U.S Constitution, only "race" is subject to strict scrutiny. Disability status is not. Thus, remedying a problem like disproportionality, which exists at the intersection of disability and race, is incredibly difficult to achieve under the current legislative framework of IDEA. Third, as Strassfeld (2016) notes, when "statutes like IDEA, along with the equal protection clause of the 14th Amendment, are [both] sources of federal rights" that states must follow and interpret when providing educational services to students with disabilities, then the "shifting balances between federal and state control" (p.1133), a form of educational federalism (Robinson, 2013 as cited in Strassfeld, 2016), generates consequential policy implementation gaps that weaken the legislation's effectiveness and affects how IDEA can be leveraged to addressed a systemic inequity like disproportionality. For instance, plaintiffs who have been affected by the issue have used intentional discrimination claims but, they "face an uphill battle in using school- and district-level placement data to prove intentional discrimination, even when policy monitoring under IDEA has led to a finding that significant disproportionality by race or ethnicity in special education and related services has occurred within the plaintiff's district. (Strassfeld, 2016, p.1140). Thus, proving that educators, a school, or district has/had an explicit intent to discriminate when disproportionate outcomes are present is a difficult and often unsuccessful claim to make and this is especially true when/if SEAs and LEAs are able to show compliance with IDEA statutes.

Collectively, these factors also reinforce the logic of compliance—legal endogeneity in particular—and deficit perspectives about the students and families who are affected by disproportionality. This is because when an SEA or an LEA can show that they have complied with IDEA and that there is no evidence of an explicit intent to discriminate, then a disparate outcome like disproportionality cannot be the fault of educators, biases and beliefs, organizational systems and failures, and/or a product of local inequities and contextual conditions. Most problematically, this reasoning allows for unequal educational outcomes to be blamed on students and families because, under the guise of compliance, educators are not explicitly discriminating against students of color with disabilities when disproportionality is present. Essentially, students have been given educational opportunities and access through compliance with IDEA and a student's lack of success in school becomes their own fault, an individual issue, rather than one that is related to broader systemic factors. This renders IDEA legislation, the indicators, and their associated compliance remedies relatively ineffective in abating a systemic inequity like disproportionality.

How then, can we approach addressing such a complex issue if there are so many barriers to achieving equity? There are no simple answers to the question but, one place to start, is for educators, policymakers, and researchers who are concerned with issues of equity in special education to become more mindful of the complex structural inequities that shape our daily lives and which influence educational systems. In addition, we must also become more aware of how our micro-decisions have macro impacts, which, despite our good intentions, contribute to educational inequalities. And, we must be willing to renounce the idea that discrimination, prejudice, and racism are only overtly conducted and blatantly obvious. We must be attuned to how we willingly, or unwillingly, take part in quiet, subversive, and insidious forms of discriminatory practices in everyday educational practice that harm students. And, we must be honest about the fact that compliance with IDEA and the guarantee of equal protection through IDEA cannot be the only measures used to assure that equity in special education is achieved. Rather, it is our duty and responsibility to push back upon the inertial forces that allow us to just "show up" (Haney Lopez, 2000) in our everyday lives and perpetuate inequities. We must be focused on combatting the unquestioned social processes that we take part in on a daily basis that contribute to the production of racial inequities. And maybe, only with this purposeful vision and commitment from multiple educational stakeholders, can we honestly pursue equity in special education and truly answer the question: Does compliance matter in special education?

Methodology

I have chosen to write a methodological appendix because I believe that a transparent detailing of my data collection and data analysis process reinforces the findings in this book. And by providing the research questions, analysis strategy, and protocols, I hope that researchers, educators, and others interested in further exploring equity issues in special education can build upon what I have shared.

This qualitative comparative ethnographic study took place over the duration of the 2011–2012 school year. It was conceptually modeled on the principles of the extended case method (Burawoy, 2009), which is a methodological orientation that links empirical data and findings to broader theoretical concepts and historical trends. The study was designed to answer the following research questions:

- In what ways does legal compliance with federal and state special education law relate to the occurrence of disproportionality?
- Is compliance with the Individuals with Disabilities Education Act (IDEA) a remedying or contributing factor to disproportionality?
- When districts are cited for being disproportionate, what drives organizational and administrative decisions and responses?
- What do district representatives, administrators, and teachers prioritize when they are trying to address a disproportionality citation, and how is this related to the social context of a district?
- How do the individual perspectives of administrators, teachers, and school personnel contribute to or sustain a specific interpretation and understanding of disproportionality?

To answer these questions, I looked at special education and disproportionality from a systemic perspective. This meant that I needed to spend time with educational leaders and see how they made sense of their educational context and how they guided their staff to address disproportionality when complying with IDEA.

FIELDWORK DETAILS

I chose to study district-level special education administrators because they communicate with their state education departments about compliance-related activities, they are responsible for initiating and enacting changes related to their districts' citations, and they oversee the majority of special education activities in schools. In the field, I spent the majority of my time following the daily activities of each district's special education administrator in his or her office, attending student special education meetings, participating in cabinet meetings with other district- and building-level administrators, attending professional development and departmental meetings, visiting and consulting with teachers, sitting in on instructional consultation meetings, and other such activities. While in these spaces, I noted how the districts were formally and informally organized (Edelman, 1992). I paid attention to how administrators followed rules and procedures and how they informally interacted with other district staff, parents, and students. I specifically noted how the informal communications between offices and positions, the behaviors of individuals in their respective positions, and informal norms and practices intersected with efforts to comply with IDEA. I also paid attention to the latent norms and biases that seemed to affect practice and influence how disproportionality and racialized outcomes were understood and rationalized within each district.

In addition to fieldwork, I conducted 26 formal interviews with district staff (e.g., secretaries, social workers, assistant superintendents, building principals). The interviews focused on understanding how staff members experienced working in the district and what their impressions were of the district's citation. The formal interviews were recorded and transcribed. I conducted 60 ad hoc informal, open-ended interviews with teachers, security guards, custodians, social workers, and building principals. These interviews were not audio-recorded, but I did take extensive notes during the interviews. I also interviewed consultants and educators who were not district staff, but were working in one of the three districts studied. All interview protocols are in Appendix C.

Lastly, I gathered meeting agendas, handouts, district forms, and local newspapers, and monitored blogs and online commentaries about the districts and school boards. These documents offered insight into the formal and informal practices of each district. Collectively, these data sources provided ample material to triangulate data and make robust conclusions about the data.

ANALYSIS STRATEGY

After exiting the field, I analyzed the data using a case-oriented approach (Miles & Huberman, 1994; Miles, Huberman, & Saldana, 2013). The approach considered each research site holistically before turning toward a broader comparative analysis. The method allows for within-case differences to be preserved when subsequent cross-case comparisons are made.

I used ATLAS.ti software to facilitate my data analysis process and reveal meanings and relationships in the mixture of fieldnotes, ad hoc interview notes, interview transcripts, publicly available district data, and field-based documents. I triangulated the multiple data sources in order to increase the validity of my findings. Through this process, I was able to compare statements made in the field and/or in interviews with other sources of information.

My analysis was carried out in three distinct phases. The first consisted of within-case district coding. I looked for trends that emerged *within* each district surrounding things such as, but not limited to, interpersonal relations; inter-professional communication; conduct of people within meetings; visitor logs to district offices; who referenced IDEA and where; how compliance with IDEA was talked about; and so forth. Using this approach I generated hundreds of inductive codes that were unique to each district. For example, a code could represent a person (labeled as a "middle school assistant principal"); a feeling (labeled as "apathy" or "building climate"); a process (labeled as "introductions"); and/or as a thing (labeled as "disproportionality indicator"). Each code was defined in a master Excel file. I did this so that I could ensure that the codes were uniformly applied within cases, and if relevant, across cases. I also consistently added new codes to the master Excel list as they emerged in the districts.

The second phase of the data analysis process consisted of *cross*-district coding. During this phase, I looked for similarities, differences, and nuances among the three districts in order to generate a broader understanding of how IDEA was implemented in each district, how a citation affected practice, and how the local context influenced district practices. I compiled a list of high-frequency codes, or codes that appeared at least 10 or more times *within* a case.

I then generated conceptually linked code families from the high-frequency codes. For example, I generated the code family "the state," from several high-frequency codes like "citation," "indicator," "state representative," "state tests," "state audit," and so forth. By conceptually linking these codes, I was able to identify data trends that I might not have seen if I had acknowledged only the individual inductively generated codes. In addition, if a high-frequency code and its subsequent code family appeared numerous times in all three districts, the concept proved to be an important conceptual point that needed further theoretical grounding. And if a high-frequency code was relevant only to one district or two districts, it provided rich analytical ground for understanding why the code was prevalent in some contexts and less so in others. Holistically, the cross-district coding process allowed me to see where the cases converged and diverged on high-frequency codes.

The third phase of the data analysis process consisted of my using the analytical notes that I had generated while proceeding through phases one and two of the data analysis to theoretically ground my findings. While coding, I had written down memos, ideas, theoretical connections, and themes that emerged throughout the analytic process. I connected these memos to relevant quotes and rich ethnographic instances that surfaced within several high-frequency codes and code families. This phase of the data analysis process provided me with the greatest insight into how my data related to sociological and critical theory and led to the findings described in this book.

SITE SELECTION AND POSITIONALITY

I chose to study suburban school districts because of findings from the Kramarczuk Voulgarides, Aylward, and Noguera (2014) study on the sociodemographic variables that contribute to the likelihood of a school district's entering and exiting a citation for disproportionality in the same large northeastern state in which I conducted the ethnography. Kramarczuk Voulgarides et al. (2014) found that geographic locale and the size of a school district influenced the probability that a school district would be cited for disproportionality and also influenced how long the district remained cited. In the study, suburban school districts had the most volatile citation histories, suggesting that there are complex social factors embedded in suburban contexts that sustain disproportionate outcomes.

I used publicly available data on school district IDEA State Performance Plans, provided by the state education department in the large northeastern state in which I conducted my research, to identify districts that would be eligible for my study. I looked for districts that had a history of disproportionality citations and that were designated as suburban school districts. Once I compiled a list of eligible school districts, I found the school district leaders' contact information (e.g., superintendent and/or district-level special education administrator) on district websites and sent letters inviting them to participate in the research project. The letters described how my project sought to understand how compliance with IDEA affected their practice when addressing disproportionality.

Five district leaders out of the 10 I contacted expressed interest in the study. Three districts agreed to participate. I had no prior direct personal or professional relationships with any of the research participants. However, I did have some professional connections with each district.

During the 2011–2012 academic year, I was working as a graduate assistant for a large urban university, in a comprehensive center (hereafter named "the Center") that focuses on addressing issues of equity within schools and districts. The Center has a very specific understanding of equity and disproportionality that is well known across the state because of their close relationship with the State Education Department and years dedicated to addressing disproportionality across the state. Although I had never directly worked with the districts that agreed to participate in the study, the Center had previously worked with two of the districts, Gerrytown and Sunderville, and had minimal contact with Huntertown.

Roger had worked with the Center for several years prior to my research. He was very frustrated with how Gerrytown operated and he appeared to want to validate his frustrations by aligning himself with the Center's mission and vision. Because of this, I would engage in conversations with him about equity. On the other hand, Huntertown had never worked with the Center. However, a technical assistance provider from the Center had participated in the state audit of the district's files after it was cited for being disproportionate. Cynthia liked the woman who had come to the audit from the Center. She often suggested that I share my experiences in Huntertown with her because Cynthia thought the district was doing a good job addressing disproportionality and she wanted everyone to know, as she often told me. Sunderville did not have a good impression of the Center. The district had previously worked with the Center but refused its assistance during the year I conducted my research. Marc often respectfully expressed dissatisfaction with the Center, and these conversations usually provided me with further insight into how he understood the district's citation. Essentially, my connection with the Center provided additional data points, which enhanced the data analysis process.

State Performance Plan
Indicators (SPP)

After the 2004 reauthorization of IDEA, the Office of Special Education Programs (OSEP) created 20 indicators to guide SEAs as they implement IDEA. The 2004 IDEA regulations pertaining to the SPP indicators are as follows:

Subpart F—Monitoring, Enforcement, Confidentiality, and Program
    Information Monitoring, Technical Assistance, and Enforcement
§ 300.600 State monitoring and enforcement.
(a) The State must monitor the implementation of this part, enforce this
    part in accordance with § 300.604(a)(1) and (a)(3), (b)(2)(i) and (b)(2)
    (v), and (c)(2), and annually report on performance under this part.
(b) The primary focus of the State's monitoring activities must be on—
    (1) Improving educational results and functional outcomes for all
        children with disabilities; and
    (2) Ensuring that public agencies meet the program requirements
        under Part B of the Act, with a particular emphasis on those
        requirements that are most closely related to improving educational
        results for children with disabilities.
(c) As a part of its responsibilities under paragraph (a) of this section, the
    State must use quantifiable indicators and such qualitative indicators
    as are needed to adequately measure performance in the priority areas
    identified in paragraph (d) of this section, and the indicators established
    by the Secretary for the State performance plans.
(d) The State must monitor the LEAs located in the State, using
    quantifiable indicators in each of the following priority areas, and
    using such qualitative indicators as are needed to adequately measure
    performance in those areas:
    (1) Provision of FAPE in the least restrictive environment.
    (2) State exercise of general supervision, including child find, effective
        monitoring, the use of resolution meetings, mediation, and a system
        of transition services as defined in § 300.43 and in 20 U.S.C.
        1437(a)(9).

(3) Disproportionate representation of racial and ethnic groups in special education and related services, to the extent the representation is the result of inappropriate identification.

The 20 State Performance Plan Indicators are listed as follows and are designed to monitor the performance of students with disabilities on each indicator:

Indicator 1: Graduation Rates

Indicator 2: Drop-Out Rates

Indicator 3: Assessment

Indicator 4: Suspension/Expulsion

Indicator 5: Least Restrictive Environment—School Age

Indicator 6: Least Restrictive Environment—Preschool

Indicator 7: Preschool Outcomes

Indicator 8: Parental Involvement

Indicator 9: Disproportionality in Special Education by Race/ Ethnicity

Indicator 10: Disproportionality in Classification/Placement by Race/ Ethnicity

Indicator 11: Child Find

Indicator 12: Early Childhood Transition

Indicator 13: Secondary Transition

Indicator 14: Post-School Outcomes

Indicator 15: Identification and Correction of Noncompliance

Indicator 16: Complaint Timelines

Indicator 17: Due Process Timelines

Indicator 18: Hearing Requests Resolved by Resolution Session

Indicator 19: Mediation Agreements

Indicator 20: State Reported Data
(*Source:* Adapted from drcvi.org/_literature_183445/Part_B_Indicators.)

For more information on how the indicators are measured, see www2. ed.gov/policy/speced/guid/idea/bapr/2014/2014-part-b-measurement-table. pdf. For a broad overview of how states have implemented and collected data for Part B and the SPP Indicators, see www2.ed.gov/fund/data/report/ idea/partbspap/allyears.html

Interview Protocols

DISTRICT STAFF INTERVIEW PROTOCOL

Research Question: In what ways does legal compliance to federal and state special education law relate to the occurrence of disproportionality?

Interviewees: School administrators, teachers, support staff, community members.

Interview Schedule: After approximately 2 months in the field, I will begin to approach relevant adults in the field about potentially participating in interviews.

Opening of Interview

Goal: To understand the interviewee's perception of the school district and community within which they work or live.

- More specifically, this interview is being conducted in order to gather information about how your district is going through or has gone through the process to address disproportionality, how this process relates to IDEA legislation, and how the compliance process affects practice in schools.
- All answers are confidential, all names will be changed, and your opinions and statements will not be shared with anyone in the school or district.
- Answer questions and help frame the interview within the larger research project objectives if needed.
- Confirm interviewee knows that I will be jotting down and taking notes as we speak. Interviews WILL NOT be recorded if the interviewee does not want it recorded.
- Confirm that interviewees can stop the interview at any time if they

would like to and that if they don't want me to use notes from their interview, I will not use them.

Interview Questions

Relationship to Community and School

1. What is your role/job in this school or district? Can you briefly describe what you do in your job or how your work relates to the school or district?
2. How many years have you worked or lived in this district?
3. What is your relationship to the community within which the school/district is located?

Impression Questions

1. What are your general impressions about the school or district within which you work?
   Probe: Can you elaborate on your answer?
   Probe: Is there something in particular that led you to your answer?
2. What are your general impressions about the larger community within which you work?
   Probe: Can you elaborate on your answer?
   Probe: Is there something in particular that led you to your answer?
3. In your opinion, would you describe your community as diverse?
   Probe: If yes, in what sense? Can you elaborate?
   Probe: If no, in what sense? Can you elaborate?

Groups in District

1. In the most general sense, how would you describe students in your district? Special education students?
   Probe: Can you elaborate on your answer?
   Probe: Can you offer some insight into why you gave your answer?
2. In the most general sense, how would you describe teachers in your district? Special education teachers?
   Probe: Can you elaborate on your answer?
   Probe: Can you offer some insight into why you gave your answer?
3. In the most general sense, how would you describe parents in your district?
   Probe: Can you elaborate on your answer?
   Probe: Can you offer some insight into why you gave your answer?

Disproportionality

1. Part of my research interest rests on understanding federal and state special education law. As per federal and state special education law, school districts must publicly announce the fact if they have had a citation for being disproportionate. Were you aware that your district has a history of being cited for disproportionality in special education?
   Probe: How did you find out? Can you elaborate on this?
   Probe: Does/did this surprise you?
   Probe: Why or why not?
   Probe: Can you elaborate on your answer?

Conclusion

Is there any more relevant information you would like to share with me about your school, district, or community?

Thank you so much for your time and candidness.

OUTSIDE ADULTS INTERVIEW PROTOCOL

Research Question: In what ways does legal compliance to federal and state special education law relate to the occurrence of disproportionality?

Interviewees: Educational professionals that are not salaried or regularly hired employees of the school district and/or serve as educational consultants in the district

Interview Schedule: After exit from the field (approximately 5 months), I will reach out to relevant adults who have done work with or in the district. Their contact information will be obtained from either encounters in the field, field informants, or through Internet searches. A general adult statement and consent form will be distributed by email or mail.

Opening of Interview

Goal: to understand the interviewee's relationship to and perception of the school district, community, special education process, and disproportionality.

- More specifically, this interview is being conducted in order to supplement ethnographic information I have gathered about the district you have worked in or currently work in. Through my ethnographic work, I noticed that your job/agency/work is related to addressing disproportionality or providing special education services in the district.

Because of this I would like to further explore and understand your perceptions of and relationship to the district.

- All answers are confidential, all names will be changed, and your opinions and statements will not be shared with anyone in the school or district.
- Answer questions and help frame the interview within the larger research project objectives if needed.
- Confirm interviewee knows that I will be jotting down and taking notes as we speak or will be tape-recording. The choice is theirs.
- Confirm that interviewees can stop the interview at any time if they would like to and that if they don't want me to use the notes of their interview, I will not use them.

Interview Questions

Professional Relationship with the District

1. What is or has been your role/job in this district?
   Probe: Can you elaborate?
   Probe: Can you please clarify?
2. Is your work extended over time? Why or why not?
3. How many years have you worked in this district?
4. What is your relationship to the community within which the school/district is located?
5. What are your general impressions about the school or district within which you work?
   Probe: Can you elaborate on your answer?
   Probe: Is there something in particular that led you to your answer?

Professional Goals and Purpose

1. Who are your "clients," or whom do you serve or advocate for?
   Probe: Can you elaborate?
2. What are your main duties or goals in your work with the district?
   Probe: Can you elaborate?
   Probe: Can you please clarify?
3. Can you describe specifically some of your work in this district?
   Probe: Can you elaborate?
4. Do you think your professional goals are met in this district? Why or why not?
   Probe: Can you please clarify?

District Contact and Personal Relationships

1. Who is/are the individual(s) most typically involved in your work with

the district? Who are your main contacts? What is the relationship like?
    Probe: Can you elaborate?
2. How would you generally describe your agency's relationship to this district?

Exploration of Impediments and Successes

1. What do you think is the most positive aspect of your work with this district in particular?
    Probe: Can you elaborate or provide further insight into your response?
    Probe: Why did you give the answer you gave?
2. What do you think is the most negative aspect of your work in this district in particular?
    Probe: Can you elaborate or provide further insight into your response?
    Probe: Why did you give the answer you gave?

Conclusion

Is there any more relevant information you would like to share with me about your work with this school, district, or community?

Thank you so much for your time and consideration.

Notes

Introduction

1. The reauthorization included: (a) guidance for states on how to monitor disproportionality; (b) guidance on the numeric formulas that could be used to identify disproportionate districts; (c) the requirement that districts found with "significant disproportionality" set aside up to 15% of IDEA funds for coordinated early-intervening services (CEIS); and (d) the requirement that state education agencies (SEAs) and local education agencies (LEAs) publicly report on the revision of policies, practices, and procedures related to IDEA implementation.

2. See Appendix B for a full list of the State Performance Plan Indicators associated with IDEA.

3. See the following link for more details on the changes to the regulations: www2. ed.gov/policy/speced/reg/idea/part-b/idea-part-b-significant-disproportionality-final-regs- changes-nprm-to-nfr.pdf

4. For more details on the delay in implementing the regulations, see www.nytimes.com/2017/12/15/us/politics/devos-obama-special-education-racial-disparities.html and civilrights.org/letter-re-enforcement-idea-provisions-regarding-significant-disproportionality/. At the time of this writing, the secretary of education has delayed them: https://www.washingtonpost.com/news/answer-sheet/wp/2018/02/26/devos-delaying-obama-era-rule-on-minority-special-education-students/?utm_term=.5b8927fc9cf2

5. See Appendix A for methodological details related to the study.

6. District names and research participant identifiers are pseudonyms. This was done to protect the identity of the research participants.

Chapter 1

1. Although the 2004 reauthorization of IDEA changed the name of the legislation to the Individuals with Disabilities Education Improvement Act (or IDEIA 2004), it remains commonly referred to as IDEA. The current iteration of IDEA requires that state and local educational agencies use federal dollars, allocated through the IDEA, to provide a free appropriate public education (FAPE) to all school-aged children labeled with a disability. School systems must provide FAPE to students with disabilities in the least restrictive environment (LRE) that is educationally appropriate in order to promote integration and reduce the seclusion of students with disabilities in schools. The legislation also mandates that states have extensive procedures and evaluations in place to screen students for a disability that are nondiscriminatory, unbiased, and involve consultation with a multidisciplinary team of

educational professionals (Kauffman & Hallahan, 2011). In addition, if a student is identified as having a disability, the school must develop an individualized education program (IEP), created in consultation with parents and a multidisciplinary team, to service the student's needs in LRE. The IEP is a confidential document that is one of the most important parts of the legislation (Kauffman & Hallahan, 2011). It is intended to be a living document wherein a student's educational and behavioral goals are created, interventions are outlined, needs are recorded and progress monitored, and high expectations are held for the student under FAPE (Yell, Shriner, & Katsiyannis, 2006). State and local education agencies (SEAs and LEAs) are required to monitor compliance with IDEA and remain in compliance with its mandates.

Chapter 2

1. Cynthia had been working for 3 months to placate a parent who did not want her child to use an iPad1 because it was "outdated and heavy." The parent threatened to sue the district if they would not provide the child with the latest version of an iPad. Cynthia and many of her staff members were very preoccupied with the parent's threat of litigation.

Chapter 5

1. See www.pbs.org/wnet/supremecourt/rights/landmark_regents.html for a brief description of the components of the *Regents of University of California v. Bakke* (1978) case.
2. Some state department of education websites promoting the use of MTSS in special education: www.nj.gov/education/njtss/overview/script.htm; www.cde.ca.gov/ci/cr/ri/mtsscomponents.asp; www.pattan.net/category/Educational%20Initiatives/Multi-Tiered%20Systems%20of%20Support%20(MTSS)

Conclusion

1. www.ed.gov/news/press-releases/fact-sheet-equity-idea
2. See the following link for the press release regarding the changes to the regulations: www2.ed.gov/policy/speced/reg/idea/part-b/idea-part-b-significant-disproportionality-final-regs- changes-nprm-to-nfr.pdf
The "Equity in IDEA" rules are listed below:

»   §§ 300.646(b) and 300.647(a) and (b) provide the standard methodology that States must use to determine whether there is significant disproportionality based on race or ethnicity in the State and its LEAs;
»   § 300.647(b)(1) requires States to set reasonable risk ratio thresholds, reasonable minimum n-sizes, reasonable minimum cell sizes, and if a State uses the flexibility described in § 300.647(d)(2), standards for measuring reasonable progress, all with input from stakeholders (including their State Advisory Panels), subject to the Department's oversight;
»   § 300.647(b)(1)(iv) sets a rebuttable presumption that a minimum cell size of no greater than 10 and a minimum n-size of no greater than 30 are reasonable.
»   § 300.647(d) provides flexibilities that States, at their discretion, may consider when determining whether significant disproportionality

exists. States may choose to identify an LEA as having significant disproportionality after an LEA exceeds a risk ratio threshold for up to three prior consecutive years. States may also choose not to identify an LEA with significant disproportionality if the LEA is making reasonable progress, as defined by the State, in lowering risk ratios in each of the two consecutive prior years, even if the risk ratios exceed the State's risk ratio thresholds;

» § 300.646(c) clarifies that the remedies in IDEA section 618(d)(2) are triggered if a State makes a determination of significant disproportionality with respect to disciplinary removals from placement;

» § 300.646(c)(1) and (2) clarify that the review of policies, practices, and procedures must occur in every year in which an LEA is identified with significant disproportionality and that LEA reporting of any revisions to policies, practices, and procedures must be in compliance with the confidentiality provisions of the Family Educational Rights and Privacy Act (FERPA), (20 U.S.C. 1232), its implementing regulations in 34 CFR part 99, and IDEA section 618(b)(1); and

» § 300.646(d) describes which populations of children may receive comprehensive CEIS when an LEA has been identified with significant disproportionality. Comprehensive CEIS may be provided to children from age 3 through grade 12, regardless of whether they are children with disabilities, and, as part of implementing comprehensive CEIS, an LEA must identify and address the factors contributing to the significant disproportionality.

3. The following timeline outlines the expected rollout of the new regulations:

» *December 2016:* "Equity in IDEA" rules are released by the U.S. Department of Education, which focus on disparities in treatment of students of color with disabilities.

» *February–July 2017:* States review the new regulations and states submit questions to the U.S. Department of Education.

» *April–December 2017:* States hold stakeholder meetings, analyze the regulations and data related to the new proposed rules, and write drafts of new state policies and procedures in reaction to the "Equity in IDEA" rules.

» *January–March 2018:* States conduct public hearings on proposed changes to policies and solicit input from the general public and key stakeholders such as the individuals with disabilities and parents of children with disabilities.

» *March–May 2019:* States make annual district-level determinations of significant disproportionality based on the new rules.

» *July 2020:* States must include determinations about students in special education that include children ages 3–5. (States have the option to include this population of students earlier if they would like.) (Source: U.S. Department of Education; www.edweek.org/ew/articles/2017/09/06/complying-with-spec-ed-bias-rule-may.html)

4. For information on the rule associated with the delay in the proposed regulations, see www.reginfo.gov/public/do/eAgendaViewRule?pubId=201710&RIN= 1820-AB77

For information on the amendment, delay, and/or elimination of the proposed regulations see: www.washingtonpost.com/news/answer-sheet/wp/2018/02/26/devos-delaying-obama-era-rule-on-minority-special-education-students/?utm_term=.5b8927fc9cf2

5. These social forces are analytically distinct yet are difficult to measure empirically. Despite this fact, the concepts have persisted and influenced organizational studies for decades (e.g., Ashworth, Boyne, & Delbridge, 2005, 2007; Mizruchi & Fein, 1999).

References

Adelman, R. M. (2005). The roles of race, class, and residential preferences in the neighborhood racial composition of middle-class blacks and whites. *Social Science Quarterly, 86*(1), 209–228.

Agirdag, O., Van Houtte, M., & Van Avermaet, P. (2012). Ethnic school segregation and self-esteem: The role of teacher-pupil relationships. *Urban Education, 47*(6), 1135–1159.

Albrecht, S. F., Skiba, R. J., Losen, D. J., Chung, C. G., & Middelberg, L. (2012). Federal policy on disproportionality in special education: Is it moving us forward? *Journal of Disability Policy Studies, 23*(1), 14–25.

Alexander, K., Entwisle, D., & Olson, L. (2014). *The long shadow: Family background, disadvantaged urban youth, and the transition to adulthood.* New York, NY: Russell Sage Foundation.

Annamma, S., Connor, D., & Ferri, B. (2013). Dis/ability critical race studies (DisCrit): Theorizing at the intersections of race and dis/ability. *Race Ethnicity and Education, 16*(1), 1–31.

Artiles, A. J. (2009). Re-framing disproportionality research: Outline of a cultural-historical paradigm. *Multiple Voices for Ethnically Diverse Exceptional Learners, 11*(2), 24–37.

Artiles, A. J. (2011). Toward an interdisciplinary understanding of educational equity and difference: The case of the racialization of ability. *Educational Researcher, 40*(9), 431–445.

Artiles, A. J. (2015). Beyond responsiveness to identity badges: Future research on culture in disability and implications for response to intervention. *Educational Review, 67*(1), 1–22.

Artiles, A. J., Bal, A., & Thorius, K. A. K. (2010). Back to the future: A critique of response to intervention's social justice views. *Theory into Practice, 49*(4), 250–257.

Artiles, A. J., Kozleski, E. B., Trent, S. C., Osher, D., & Ortiz, A. (2010). Justifying and explaining disproportionality, 1968–2008: A critique of underlying views of culture. *Exceptional Children, 76*(3), 279–299.

Artiles, A. J., Rueda, R., Salazar, J. J., & Higareda, I. (2005). Within-group diversity in minority disproportionate representation: English language learners in urban school districts. *Exceptional Children, 71*(3), 283–300.

Arum, R. (2000). Schools and communities: Ecological and institutional dimensions. *Annual Review of Sociology, 26*(1), 395–418.

Ashworth, R., Boyne, G., & Delbridge, R. (2005). Institutional pressures on public organizations: An empirical test of isomorphism. *Management Research Review*, *28*(9), 61.

Ashworth, R., Boyne, G., & Delbridge, R. (2007). Escape from the iron cage? Organizational change and isomorphic pressures in the public sector. *Journal of Public Administration Research and Theory*, *19*(1), 165–187.

Averill, O. H., & Rinaldi, C. (2011). Multi-tier system of supports (MTSS). *District Administration*, *48*(8), 91–95.

Bal, A., Kozleski, E. B., Schrader, E. M., Rodriguez, E. M., & Pelton, S. (2014). Systemic transformation from the ground–up: Using learning lab to design culturally responsive schoolwide positive behavioral supports. *Remedial and Special Education*, *35*(6), 327–339.

Bal, A., Thorius, K. K., & Kozleski, E. (2012). *Culturally responsive positive behavioral support matters*. Tempe, AZ: The Equity Alliance.

Beck, A., & Muschkin, C. (2012). The enduring impact of race: Understanding disparities in student disciplinary infractions and achievement. *Sociological Perspectives*, *55*(4), 637–662.

Blanchett, W. J. (2010). Telling it like it is: The role of race, class, & culture in the perpetuation of learning disability as a privileged category for the white middle class. *Disability Studies Quarterly*, *30*(2).

Blau, P., & Duncan, O. D. (1967). *The American occupational structure*. New York, NY: John Wiley & Sons.

Blue-Banning, M., Summers, J. A., Frankland, H. C., Nelson, L. L., & Beegle, G. (2004). Dimensions of family and professional partnerships: Constructive guidelines for collaboration. *Exceptional children*, *70*(2), 167–184.

Bohrnstedt, G., Kitmitto, S., Ogut, B., Sherman, D., & Chan, D. (2015). *School composition and the Black-White achievement gap*. NCES 2015-018. National Center for Education Statistics.

Bonilla-Silva, E. (1997). Rethinking racism: Toward a structural interpretation. *American sociological review*, 465–480.

Bonilla-Silva, E. (2015). More than prejudice: Restatement, reflections, and new directions in critical race theory. *Sociology of Race and Ethnicity*, *1*(1), 73–87.

Bonilla-Silva, E. (2017). *Racism without racists: Color-blind racism and the persistence of racial inequality in America*. New York, NY: Rowman & Littlefield.

Bouman, S. H. (2010). Response-to-intervention in California public schools: Has it helped address disproportional placement rates for students with learning disabilities? (Dissertation). Claremont, CA: The Claremont Graduate University.

Bourdieu, P. (1977). *Outline of a theory of practice* (Cambridge Studies in Social and Cultural Anthropology, Vol. 16). Cambridge, United Kingdom: Cambridge University Press.

Bourdieu, P., & Passeron, J. C. (1977). *Reproduction in society, education and culture* (R. Nice, Trans.) London, United Kingdom: Sage.

Bowker, G. C., & Star, S. L. (2000). *Sorting things out: Classification and its consequences*. Cambridge, MA: MIT Press.

Boykin, A. W., & Noguera, P. (2011). *Creating the opportunity to learn: Moving from research to practice to close the achievement gap*. Alexandria, VA: ASCD.

Bryk, A. S., Sebring, P. B., Allensworth, E., Luppescu, S., & Easton, J. Q. (2010). *Organizing schools for improvement: Lessons from Chicago*. Chicago, IL: University of Chicago Press.

Buchmann, C., & DiPrete, T. A. (2006). The growing female advantage in college completion: The role of family background and academic achievement. *American Sociological Review, 71*(4), 515–541.

Burawoy, M. (2009). *The extended case method: Four countries, four decades, four great transformations, and one theoretical tradition.* Berkeley, CA: University of California Press.

Burke, M. A. (2016). New frontiers in the study of color-blind racism: A materialist approach. *Social Currents, 3*(2), 103–109.

Burke, M. A. (2017). Colorblind racism: Identities, ideologies, and shifting subjectivities. *Sociological Perspectives, 60*(5), 857–865.

Carter, P. L. (2013). Student and school cultures and the opportunity gap. In P. L. Carter & K. G. Welner (Eds.), *Closing the opportunity gap: What America must do to give every child an even chance, 143–155.* New York, NY: Oxford University Press.

Carter, P. L., & Welner, K. G. (Eds.). (2013). *Closing the opportunity gap: What America must do to give every child an even chance.* New York, NY: Oxford University Press.

Cavendish, W., Artiles, A. J., & Harry, B. (2014). Tracking inequality 60 years after Brown: Does policy legitimize the racialization of disability? *Multiple Voices for Ethnically Diverse Exceptional Learners, 14*(2), 30–40.

Colvin, G., Sugai, G., Good, R. H. III, & Lee, Y. Y. (1997). Using active supervision and pre-correction to improve transition behaviors in an elementary school. *School Psychology Quarterly, 12,* 344–363.

Connor, D. J., Ferri, B. A., & Annamma, S. A. (Eds.). (2016). *DisCrit—Disability studies and critical race theory in education.* New York, NY: Teachers College Press.

Cooper, C. W. (2009). Performing cultural work in demographically changing schools: Implications for expanding transformative leadership frameworks. *Educational Administration Quarterly, 45*(5), 694–724.

Coutinho, M. J., Oswald, D. P., Best, A. M., & Forness, S. R. (2002). Gender and sociodemographic factors and the disproportionate identification of culturally and linguistically diverse students with emotional disturbance. *Behavioral Disorders, 27*(2), 109–125.

Darling-Hammond, L. (2004). Inequality and the right to learn: Access to qualified teachers in California's public schools. *Teachers College Record, 106*(10), 1936–1966.

Darling-Hammond, L. (2013). Inequality and school resources. In P. L. Carter & K. G. Welner (Eds.), *Closing the opportunity gap: What America must do to give every child an even chance* (p. 77). New York, NY: Oxford University Press.

Delgado, R. (1990). When a story is just a story: Does voice really matter? *Virginia Law Review,* 95–111.

Delpit, L. (2006). *Other people's children: Cultural conflict in the classroom.* New York, NY: The New Press.

DiMaggio, P., & Powell, W. W. (1983). The iron cage revisited: Collective rationality and institutional isomorphism in organizational fields. *American Sociological Review, 48*(2), 147–160.

Doane, A. (2017). Beyond color-blindness: (Re)theorizing racial ideology. *Sociological Perspectives, 60*(5), 975–991.

Donovan, S. M., & Cross, C. T. (2002). *Minority students in special and gifted education*. Washington, DC: National Academies Press.

Dumais, S. A. (2002). Cultural capital, gender, and school success: The role of habitus. *Sociology of Education, 75*(1), 44–68.

Dunn, L. M. (1968). Special education for the mildly retarded: Is much of it justifiable? *Exceptional children, 34,* 5–22.

Edelman, L. B. (1990). Legal environments and organizational governance: The expansion of due process in the American workplace. *American Journal of Sociology, 95*(6), 1401–1440.

Edelman, L. B. (1992). Legal ambiguity and symbolic structures: Organizational mediation of civil rights law. *American Journal of Sociology, 97*(6), 1531–1576.

Edelman, L. B., Krieger, L. H., Eliason, S. R., Albiston, C. R., & Mellema, V. (2011). When organizations rule: Judicial deference to institutionalized employment structures. *American Journal of Sociology, 117*(3), 888–954.

Education for All Handicapped Children Act, 20 U.S.C. § 1418 (1975).

Eitle, T. M. (2002). Special education or racial segregation: Understanding variation in the representation of Black students in educable mentally handicapped programs. *Sociological Quarterly, 43*(4), 575–605.

Elhoweris, H., Mutua, K., Alsheikh, N., & Holloway, P. (2005). Effect of children's ethnicity on teachers' referral and recommendation decisions in gifted and talented programs. *Remedial and Special Education, 26*(1), 25–31.

Engeström, Y. (2011). From design experiments to formative interventions. *Theory & Psychology, 21*(5), 598–628.

Evans, A. E. (2007). Changing faces: Suburban school response to demographic change. *Education and Urban Society, 39*(3), 315–348.

Fairbanks, S., Sugai, G., Guardino, D., & Lathrop, M. (2007). Response to intervention: Examining classroom behavior support in second grade. *Exceptional Children, 73,* 288–310.

Fergus, E. (2016). *Solving disproportionality and achieving equity: A leader's guide to using data to change hearts and minds*. Thousand Oaks, CA: Corwin Press.

Finn, Jr., C. E., Rotherham, A. J., & Hokanson, Jr., C. R. (2001). *Rethinking special education for a new century*. Washington, DC: Thomas B. Fordham Foundation and the Progressive Policy Institute.

Finn, J. D. (1982). Patterns in special education placement as revealed by the OCR surveys. In National Research Council, *Placing children in special education: A strategy for equity* (pp. 322–381). Washington, DC: National Academies Press.

Foot, K. A. (2001). Cultural-historical activity theory as practice theory: Illuminating the development of conflict-monitoring network. *Communication Theory, 11*(1), 56–83.

Ford, D. Y. (1998). The underrepresentation of minority students in gifted education problems and promises in recruitment and retention. *Journal of Special Education, 32*(1), 4–14.

Ford, D. Y., Scott, M. T., Moore, J. L., & Amos, S. O. (2013). Gifted education and culturally different students examining prejudice and discrimination via microaggressions. *Gifted Child Today, 36*(3), 205–208.

Fordham, S., & Ogbu, J. U. (1986). Black students' school success: Coping with the "burden of 'acting white.'" *Urban Review, 18*(3), 176–206.

Frankenberg, E., & Orfield, G. (2012). *The resegregation of suburban schools.* Cambridge, MA: Harvard Educational Press.

Frey, W. (2011). *Melting pot cities and suburbs: Racial and ethnic change in metro America in the 2000s.* Washington, DC: The Brookings Institution.

Fry, R. (2009). *The rapid growth and changing complexion of suburban public schools.* Washington, DC: Pew Hispanic Center.

Garcia, S. B., & Guerra, P. L. (2004). Deconstructing deficit thinking: Working with educators to create more equitable learning environments. *Education and urban society, 36*(2), 150–168.

García, S. B., Mendez Perez, A., & Ortiz, A. A. (2000). Mexican American mothers' beliefs about disabilities: Implications for early childhood intervention. *Remedial and Special Education, 21*(2), 90–120.

Gay, G. (2010). *Culturally responsive teaching: Theory, research, and practice.* New York, NY: Teachers College Press.

Gorski, P. C. (2015). *Reaching and teaching students in poverty: Strategies for erasing the opportunity gap.* New York, NY: Teachers College Press.

Gregory, A., & Weinstein, R. S. (2008). The discipline gap and African Americans: Defiance or cooperation in the high school classroom. *Journal of School Psychology, 46*(4), 455–475.

Guinier, L., & Torres, G. (2003). *The miner's canary: Enlisting race, resisting power, transforming democracy.* Cambridge, MA: Harvard University Press.

Gutiérrez, K. D. (2008). Developing a sociocritical literacy in the third space. *Reading Research Quarterly, 43*(2), 148–164.

Gutiérrez, K. D., Larson, J., Enciso, P., & Ryan, C. L. (2007). Discussing expanded spaces for learning. *Language Arts, 85*(1), 69.

Haney Lopez, I. F. (2000). Institutional racism: Judicial conduct and a new theory of racial discrimination. *Yale Law Journal, 109*, 1717–1884.

Haney Lopez, I. F. (2009). *Racism on trial: The Chicano fight for justice.* Cambridge, MA: Harvard University Press.

Harris III, J. J., & Ford, D. Y. (1999). Hope deferred again: Minority students underrepresented in gifted programs. *Education and Urban Society, 31*(2), 225–37.

Harris, C. I. (1993). Whiteness as property. *Harvard Law Review, 106*(8), 1707–1791.

Harris, C. I. (2000). Equal treatment and the reproduction of inequality. *Fordham Law Review, 69*, 1753.

Harry, B. (2002). Trends and issues in serving culturally diverse families of children with disabilities. *Journal of Special Education, 36*(3), 132–140.

Harry, B. (2008). Collaboration with culturally and linguistically diverse families: Ideal versus reality. *Exceptional Children, 74*(3), 372–388.

Harry, B., Allen, N., & McLaughlin, M. (1995). Communication versus compliance: African-American parents' involvement in special education. *Exceptional Children, 61*(4), 364–377.

Harry, B., & Anderson, M. G. (1994). The disproportionate placement of African American males in special education programs: A critique of the process. *Journal of Negro Education, 63*(4), 602–619.

Harry, B., & Klingner, J. (2014). *Why are so many minority students in special education?* (2nd ed.) New York, NY: Teachers College Press.

Harry, B., Klingner, J. K., & Hart, J. (2005). African American families under fire: Ethnographic views of family strengths. *Remedial and Special Education*, 26(2), 101–112.

Hauser, R. M., Tsai, S. L., & Sewell, W. H. (1983). A model of stratification with response error in social and psychological variables. *Sociology of Education*, 56(1), 20–46.

Heck, A., Collins, J., & Peterson, L. (2001) Decreasing children's risk taking on the playground. *Journal of Applied Behavior Analysis*, 34(3), 349–352.

Hehir, T. (2002). IDEA and disproportionality: Federal enforcement, effective advocacy, and strategies for change. In D. Losen & G. Orfield (Eds.), *Racial inequity in special education* (pp. 219–238). Cambridge, MA: Harvard Education Publishing Group.

Holme, J. J., Diem, S., & Welton, A. (2014). Suburban school districts and demographic change: The technical, normative, and political dimensions of response. *Educational Administration Quarterly*, 50(1), 34–66.

Hout, M. (1988). More universalism, less structural mobility: The American occupational structure in the 1980s. *American Journal of Sociology*, 93(6), 1358–1400.

Hout, M., & DiPrete, T. A. (2006). What we have learned: RC28's contributions to knowledge about social stratification. *Research in Social Stratification and Mobility*, 24(1), 1–20.

Hyman, E., Rivkin, D. H., & Rosenbaum, S. A. (2011). How IDEA fails families without means: Causes and corrections from the frontlines of special education lawyering. *American University Journal of Gender, Social Policy & the Law*, 20(1), 107–162.

Ingram, K., Lewis-Palmer, T., & Sugai, G. (2005). Function-based intervention planning comparing the effectiveness of FBA function-based and non-function-based intervention plans. *Journal of Positive Behavior Interventions*, 7, 224–236.

Irvine, J. J. (1992). Making teacher education culturally responsive. In M. E. Dilworth (Ed.), *Diversity in teacher education: New expectations* (pp. 79–92). San Francisco, CA: Jossey-Bass.

Jimerson, S. R., Burns, M. K., & VanDerHeyden, A. M. (2016). From response to intervention to multi-tiered systems of support: Advances in the science and practice of assessment and intervention. In *Handbook of Response to Intervention* (pp. 1–6). New York, NY: Springer US.

Jones, C., Caravaca, L., Cizek, S., Horner, R., & Vincent, C. (2010). Culturally responsive schoolwide positive behavior support: A case study in one school with a high proportion of Native American students. *Multiple Voices for Ethnically Diverse Exceptional Learners*, 9(1), 108–119.

Kalyanpur, M., Harry, B., & Skrtic, T. (2000). Equity and advocacy expectations of culturally diverse families' participation in special education. *International Journal of Disability, Development and Education*, 47(2), 119–136.

Kartub, D. T., Taylor-Greene, S., March, R. E., & Horner, R. H. (2000). Reducing hallway noise: A systems approach. *Journal of Positive Behavior Interventions*, 2, 179–182.

Kauffman, J. M., & Hallahan, D. P. (Eds.). (2011). *Handbook of special education*. New York, NY: Routledge.

Kim, C. Y., Losen, D. J., & Hewitt, D. T. (2010). *The school-to-prison pipeline: Structuring legal reform*. New York, NY: NYU Press.

Klingner, J., Artiles, A. J., Kozleski, E., Harry, B., Zion, S., Tate, W., . . . & Riley, D. (2005). Addressing the disproportionate representation of culturally and linguistically diverse students in special education through culturally responsive educational systems. *Education Policy Analysis Archives/Archivos Analíticos de Políticas Educativas, 13*(38).

Kozleski, E. B., Engelbrecht, P., Hess, R., Swart, E., Eloff, I., Oswald, M., . . . & Jain, S. (2008). Where differences matter: A cross-cultural analysis of family voice in special education. *Journal of Special Education, 42*(1), 26–35.

Kozleski, E. B., Sobel, D., & Taylor, S. (2003). Embracing and building culturally responsive practices. *Multiple Voices for Ethnically Diverse Exceptional Learners, 6*(1), 73–87.

Kozleski, E. B., & Zion, S. (2006). Preventing disproportionality by strengthening district policies and procedures—an assessment and strategic planning process. Retrieved from www.researchgate.net/publication/296706566_Preventing_DISPROPORTIONALITY_by_Strengthening_District_Policies_and_Procedures_-_An_Assessment_and_Strategic_Planning_Process

Kramarczuk Voulgarides, C., Aylward, A., & Noguera, P. A. (2014). Elusive quest for equity: An analysis of how contextual factors contribute to the likelihood of school districts being legally cited for racial disproportionality in special education. *Journal of Law and Society, 15*, 241.

Kramarczuk Voulgarides, C., Fergus, E., & Thorius, K. A. K. (2017). Pursuing equity: Disproportionality in special education and the reframing of technical solutions to address systemic inequities. *Review of Research in Education, 41*(1), 61–87.

Kramarczuk Voulgarides, C., Zwerger, N., & Noguera, P. *Identifying the root causes of disproportionality.* Retrieved from steinhardt.nyu.edu/scmsAdmin/media/users/ll81/Identifying_the_Root_Causes_of_Disproportionality.pdf

Kuchle, L. B., Zumeta Edmonds, R., Danielson, L. C., Peterson, A., & Riley Tillman, T. C. (2015). The next big idea: A framework for integrated academic and behavioral intensive intervention. *Learning Disabilities Research & Practice, 30*(4), 150–158.

Kummerer, S. E., & Lopez-Reyna, N. A. (2009). Engaging Mexican immigrant families in language and literacy interventions: Three case studies. *Remedial and Special Education, 30*(6), 330–343.

Ladson-Billings, G. (1995a). But that's just good teaching! The case for culturally relevant pedagogy. *Theory into Practice, 34*(3), 159–165.

Ladson-Billings, G. (1995b). Toward a theory of culturally relevant pedagogy. *American Educational Research Journal, 32*(3), 465–491.

Ladson-Billings, G. (2001). *Crossing over to Canaan: The journey of new teachers in diverse classrooms.* San Francisco, CA: Jossey-Bass.

Ladson-Billings, G. (2006). From the achievement gap to the education debt: Understanding achievement in U.S. schools. *Educational Researcher, 35*(7), 3–12.

Lareau, A. (2002). Invisible inequality: Social class and childrearing in black families and white families. *American Sociological Review*, 747–776.

Lareau, A. (2011). *Unequal childhoods: Class, race, and family life.* Berkeley, CA: University of California Press.

Leedy, A., Bates, P., & Safran, S. P. (2004). Bridging the research-to-practice gap: Improving hallway behavior using positive behavior supports. *Behavioral Disorders, 29*, 130–139.

Leithwood, K., Seashore-Louis, K., Anderson, S., & Wahlstrom, K. (2004). *Executive summary: How leadership influences student learning.* Learning From Leadership Project, The Wallace Foundation. Retrieved from www.wallace-foundation.org/knowledge-center/pages/executive-summary-how-leadership-influences-student-learning.aspx

Leonardo, Z., & Broderick, A. (2011). Smartness as property: A critical exploration of intersections between whiteness and disability studies. *Teachers College Record, 113*(10), 2206–2232.

Lewis, A. E. (2001). There is no "race" in the schoolyard: Color-blind ideology in an (almost) all-white school. *American Educational Research Journal, 38*(4), 781–811.

Lewis, A. E. (2003). *Race in the schoolyard: Negotiating the color line in classrooms and communities.* New Brunswick, NJ: Rutgers University Press.

Lewis, T. J., Colvin, G., & Sugai, G. (2000). The effects of precorrection and active supervision on the recess behavior of elementary school students. *Education and Treatment of Children, 23,* 109–121.

Lewis, T. J., Sugai, G., & Colvin, G. (1998). Reducing problem behavior through a school-wide system of effective behavior support: Investigation of a school-wide social skills training program and contextual interventions. *School Psychology Review, 27,* 446–460.

Lewis-McCoy, R. H. (2014). *Inequality in the promised land: Race, resources, and suburban schooling.* Palo Alto, CA: Stanford University Press.

Losen, D. J. (Ed.). (2014). *Closing the school discipline gap: Equitable remedies for excessive exclusion.* New York, NY: Teachers College Press.

Losen, D. J., & Orfield, G. (2002). *Racial inequity in special education.* Cambridge, MA: Harvard Education Publishing Group.

Louis, K. S., Leithwood, K., Wahlstrom, K. L., Anderson, S. E., Michlin, M., & Mascall, B. (2010). *Learning from leadership: Investigating the links to improved student learning.* Center for Applied Research and Educational Improvement/University of Minnesota and Ontario Institute for Studies in Education/University of Toronto. Retrieved from www.wallacefoundation.org/knowledge-center/Documents/Investigating-the-Links-to-Improved-Student-Learning.pdf

Lucas, S. R. (2001). Effectively maintained inequality: Education transitions, track mobility, and social background effects. *American Journal of Sociology, 106*(6), 1642–1690.

MacLeod, J. (2008). *Ain't no makin' it: Aspirations and attainment in a low-income neighborhood.* Boulder, CO: Westview Press.

Maheady, L., Towne, R., Algozzine, B., Mercer, J., & Ysseldyke, J. (1983). Minority overrepresentation: A case for alternative practices prior to referral. *Learning Disability Quarterly, 6*(4), 448–456.

March, J. G., & Simon, H. A. (1958). *Organizations.* New York, NY: John Wiley & Sons.

Mare, R. D., & Maralani, V. (2006). The intergenerational effects of changes in women's educational attainments. *American Sociological Review, 71*(4), 542–564.

Markowitz, J. (2002, February). *State criteria for determining disproportionality. Quick Turn Around (QTA).* Retrieved from archive.org/details/ERIC_ED462810

Martinez, A. A., McMahon, S. D., & Treger, S. (2016). Individual- and school-level predictors of student office disciplinary referrals. *Journal of Emotional & Behavioral Disorders, 24*(1), 30–41.

McCall, Z., & Skrtic, T. (2009). Intersectional needs politics: A policy frame for the wicked problem of disproportionality. *Multiple Voices for Ethnically Diverse Exceptional Learners, 11*(2), 3–23.

McKinney, E., Bartholomew, C., & Gray, L. (2010). RTI and SWPBIS: Confronting the problem of disproportionality. *Communique, 38*(6), 1, 26, 28–29.

Mehan, H. (1992). Understanding inequality in schools: The contribution of interpretive studies. *Sociology of Education, 65*(1), 1–20.

Mehan, H., Hertweck, A., & Meihls, J. L. (1986). *Handicapping the handicapped: Decision making in students' educational careers*. Palo Alto, CA: Stanford University Press.

Mendoza, E., Paguyo, C. H., & Gutiérrez, K. D. (2015). Understanding the intersection of race and dis/ability through common sense notions of learning and culture. In D. Connor, B. Ferri, & S. Annamma (Eds.), *DisCrit: Disability studies and critical race theory in education* (pp. 71–86). New York, NY: Teachers College Press.

Meyer, J. W., & Rowan, B. (1977). Institutionalized organizations: Formal structure as myth and ceremony. *American Journal of Sociology, 83*(2), 340–363.

Miles, M. B., & Huberman, A. M. (1994). *Qualitative data analysis: An expanded sourcebook*. Thousand Oaks, CA: Sage.

Miles, M. B., Huberman, A. M., & Saldana, J. (2013). *Qualitative data analysis*. Thousand Oaks, CA: Sage.

Milner IV, H. R. (2010). *Start where you are, but don't stay there: Understanding diversity, opportunity gaps, and teaching in today's classrooms*. Cambridge, MA: Harvard Education Press.

Minow, M. (2010). *In Brown's wake: Legacies of America's educational landmark*. New York, NY: Oxford University Press.

Mizruchi, M. S., & Fein, L. C. (1999). The social construction of organizational knowledge: A study of the uses of coercive, mimetic, and normative isomorphism. *Administrative Science Quarterly, 44*(4), 653–683.

Moreno, G., & Bullock, L. M. (2011). Principles of positive behavior supports: Using the FBA as a problem-solving approach to address challenging behaviors beyond special populations. *Emotional & Behavioral Difficulties, 16*, 117–127.

Mrazek, P. J., & Haggerty, R. J. (Eds.). (1994). *Reducing risks for mental disorders: Frontiers for preventive intervention research*. Washington, DC: National Academies Press.

Murillo, E. G. (2002). How does it feel to be a problem?: "Disciplining" the transnational subject in the American South. In S. Wortham, E. Murillo, & E. Hamann (Eds.), *Education in the new Latino diaspora: Policy and the politics of identity* (pp. 215–240). Westport, CT: Ablex Publishing.

National Research Council. (2002). *Minority students in special and gifted education*. Washington, DC: National Academies Press.

Neal, L. V. I., McCray, A. D., Webb-Johnson, G., & Bridgest, S. T. (2003). The effects of African American movement styles on teachers' perceptions and reactions. *The Journal of Special Education, 37*(1), 49–57.

Nelson, J. R., Colvin, G., & Smith, D. J. (1996, Summer/Fall). The effects of setting clear standards on students' social behavior in common areas of the school. *Journal of At-Risk Issues, 3,* 10–18.

Newcomer, L. L., & Lewis, T. J. (2004). Functional behavioral assessment: An investigation of assessment reliability and effectiveness of function-based interventions. *Journal of Emotional and Behavioral Disorders, 12,* 168–181.

Oakes, J. (2005). *Keeping track: How schools structure inequality.* New Haven, CT: Yale University Press.

Oakes, J., Quartz, K. H., Gong, J., Guiton, G., & Lipton, M. (1993). Creating middle schools: Technical, normative, and political considerations. *Elementary School Journal, 93*(5), 461–480.

Oakes, J., Welner, K., Yonezawa, S., & Allen, R. (2005). Norms and politics of equity-minded change: Researching the "zone of mediation." In M. Fullan (Ed.), *Fundamental change: International handbook on educational change* (pp. 282–305). Dordrecht, Netherlands: Springer.

Obasogie, O. (2013). *Blinded by sight: Seeing race through the eyes of the blind.* Palo Alto, CA: Stanford University Press.

Ogbu, J. U. (1979). *Minority education and caste: The American system in cross-cultural perspective. Crisis, 86*(1), 17–21.

Ogbu, J. U. (1987). Variability in minority school performance: A problem in search of an explanation. *Anthropology & Education Quarterly, 18*(4), 312–334.

Ong-Dean, C. (2009). *Distinguishing disability: Parents, privilege, and special education.* Chicago, IL: University of Chicago Press.

Ong-Dean, C., Daly, A. J., & Park, V. (2011). Privileged advocates: Disability and education policy in the USA. *Policy Futures in Education, 9*(3), 392–405.

Orfield, M. (2002). *American metropolitics.* Washington, DC: Urban Institute Press.

Oswald, D. P., & Coutinho, M. J. (1995). Identification and placement of students with serious emotional disturbance. Part I: Correlates of state child-count data. *Journal of Emotional and Behavioral Disorders, 3*(4), 224–229.

Oswald, D. P., Coutinho, M. J., & Best, A. M. (2002). Community and school predictors of overrepresentation of minority children in special education. *Racial Inequity in Special Education,* 1–13.

Oswald, D. P., Coutinho, M. J., Best, A. M., & Nguyen, N. (2001). Impact of sociodemographic characteristics on the identification rates of minority students as having mental retardation. *Mental Retardation, 39*(5), 351–367.

Oswald, D. P., Coutinho, M. J., Best, A. M., & Singh, N. N. (1999). Ethnic representation in special education: The influence of school-related economic and demographic variables. *The Journal of Special Education, 32*(4), 194–206.

Paris, D., & Alim, H. S. (2014). What are we seeking to sustain through culturally sustaining pedagogy? A loving critique forward. *Harvard Educational Review, 84*(1), 85–100.

Paris, D., & Alim, H. S. (Eds.). (2017). *Culturally sustaining pedagogies: Teaching and learning for justice in a changing world.* New York, NY: Teachers College Press.

Parrish, T. B. (2002). Racial disparities in the identification, funding, and provision of special education. In D. J. Losen & G. Orfield (Eds.), *Racial inequity in special education,* (pp. 15–37). Cambridge, MA: Harvard Education Publishing Group.

Parrish, T. B., & Wolman, J. (2004). How is special education funded?: Issues and implications for school administrators. *NASSP Bulletin*, *88*(640), 57–68.

Payne, C. M. (1984). *Getting what we ask for: The ambiguity of success and failure in urban education*. Westport, CT: Greenwood Press.

Pazey, B. L., & Cole, H. A. (2013). The role of special education training in the development of socially just leaders: Building an equity consciousness in educational leadership programs. *Educational Administration Quarterly*, *49*(2), 243–271.

Peterson, E. R., Rubie-Davies, C. M., Elley-Brown, M. J., Widdowson, D. A., Dixon, R. S., & Irving, S. E. (2011). Who is to blame? Students, teachers and parents views on who is responsible for student achievement. *Research in Education*, *86*(1), 1–12.

Pettigrew, T. F. (2004). Justice deferred a half century after *Brown v. Board of Education*. *American Psychologist*, *59*(6), 521.

Pollock, M. (2004). Race wrestling: Struggling strategically with race in educational practice and research. *American Journal of Education*, *111*(1), 25–67.

Pollock, M. (2009). *Colormute: Race talk dilemmas in an American school*. Princeton, NJ: Princeton University Press.

Pollock, M. (2010). *Because of race: How Americans debate harm and opportunity in our schools*. Princeton, NJ: Princeton University Press.

Pollock, M., Deckman, S., Mira, M., & Shalaby, C. (2010). "But what can I do?": Three necessary tensions in teaching teachers about race. *Journal of Teacher Education*, *61*(3), 211–224.

Putnam, R. F., Handler, M. W., Ramirez-Platt, C., & Luiselli, J. K. (2003). Improving student bus riding behavior through a whole-school intervention. *Journal of Applied Behavior Analysis*, *36*, 583–589.

Renee, M., Welner, K., & Oakes, J. (2010). Social movement organizing and equity-focused educational change: Shifting the zone of mediation. In *Second international handbook of educational change* (pp. 153–168). Cham, Switzerland: Springer International.

Rutherford, R. B., Bullis, M., Anderson, C. W., & Griller-Clark, H. M. (2002). *Youth with disabilities in the correctional system: Prevalence rates and identification issues*. Washington, DC: Office of Juvenile Justice and Delinquency Prevention.

Saito, L. T. (2009). *The politics of exclusion: The failure of race-neutral policies in urban America*. Palo Alto, CA: Stanford University Press.

Samson, J. F., & Lesaux, N. K. (2009). Language minority learners in special education: Rates and predictors of identification for services. *Journal of Learning Disabilities*, *42*, 148–162.

Sewell, W. H., & Shah, V. P. (1967). Socioeconomic status, intelligence, and the attainment of higher education. *Sociology of Education*, *40*, 1–23.

Sewell, W. H., Haller, A. O., & Portes, A. (1969). The educational and early occupational attainment process. *American Sociological Review*, 82–92.

Sieber, S. (1981). *Fatal remedies*. New York, NY: Plenum.

Sieber, S. (2013). *Fatal remedies: The ironies of social intervention*. Springer Science & Business Media.

Skiba, R. J. (2013). CCBD'S position summary on federal policy on disproportionality in special education. *Behavioral Disorders*, *38*(2).

Skiba, R. J., Chung, C. G., Trachok, M., Baker, T. L., Sheya, A., & Hughes, R. L. (2014). Parsing disciplinary disproportionality: Contributions of infraction, student, and school characteristics to out-of-school suspension and expulsion. *American Educational Research Journal, 51*(4), 640–670.

Skiba, R. J., Horner, R. H., Chung, C. G., Rausch, M. K., May, S. L., & Tobin, T. (2011). Race is not neutral: A national investigation of African American and Latino disproportionality in school discipline. *School Psychology Review, 40,* 85–107.

Skiba, R. J., Poloni-Staudinger, L., Simmons, A. B., Renae Feggins-Azziz, L., & Chung, C. G. (2005). Unproven links: Can poverty explain ethnic disproportionality in special education? *Journal of Special Education, 39*(3), 130–144.

Skiba, R. J., Simmons, A. B., Ritter, S., Gibb, A. C., Rausch, M. K., Cuadrado, J., & Chung, C. G. (2008). Achieving equity in special education: History, status, and current challenges. *Exceptional Children, 74*(3), 264–288.

Skiba, R., Simmons, A., Ritter, S., Kohler, K., Henderson, M., & Wu, T. (2006). The context of minority disproportionality: Practitioner perspectives on special education referral. *Teachers College Record, 108*(7), 1424–1459.

Skrentny, J. D. (2009). *The minority rights revolution.* Cambridge, MA: Harvard University Press.

Skrla, L., Scheurich, J. J., Garcia, J., & Nolly, G. (2004). Equity audits: A practical leadership tool for developing equitable and excellent schools. *Educational Administration Quarterly, 40*(1), 133–161.

Smith, C. W., & Mayorga-Gallo, S. (2017). The new principle-policy gap: How diversity ideology subverts diversity initiatives. *Sociological Perspectives, 60*(5), 889–911.

Spaulding, L. S., & Pratt, S. M. (2015). A review and analysis of the history of special education and disability advocacy in the United States. *American Educational History Journal, 42*(1/2), 91.

Stein, E. B. (2009, May). The Individuals with Disabilities Education Act (IDEA): Judicial remedies for systemic noncompliance. *Wisconsin Law Review,* 801.

Sterman, J. D. (1994). Learning in and about complex systems. *System Dynamics Review, 10*(2-3), 291–330.

Strassfeld, N. M. (2016). The future of idea: monitoring disproportionate representation of minority students in special education and intentional discrimination claims. *Case Western Reserve Law Review, 67,* 1121.

Sullivan, A. L. (2011). Disproportionality in special education identification and placement of English language learners. *Exceptional Children, 77*(3), 317–334.

Sullivan, A. L., & Artiles, A. J. (2011). Theorizing racial inequity in special education: Applying structural inequity theory to disproportionality. *Urban Education, 46*(6), 1526–1552.

Sullivan, A. L., Artiles, A. J., & Hernandez-Saca, D. I. (2015). Addressing special education inequity through systemic change: Contributions of ecologically based organizational consultation. *Journal of Educational and Psychological Consultation, 25*(2–3), 129–147.

Sullivan, A. L., Klingbeil, D. A., & Van Norman, E. R. (2013). Beyond behavior: Multilevel analysis of the influence of sociodemographics and school characteristics on students' risk of suspension. *School Psychology Review, 42*(1), 99.

Thorius, K. A. K., Maxcy, B. D., Macey, E., & Cox, A. (2014). A critical practice analysis of response to intervention appropriation in an urban school. *Remedial and Special Education, 35*(5), 287–299.

Thorius, K. A. K., & Tan, P. (2015). Expanding analysis of educational debt: Considering intersections of race and ability. In D. Connor, B. Ferri & S. A. Annamma (Eds.), *DisCrit: Critical conversations across race, class, & dis/ability* (pp. 87–97). New York, NY: Teachers College Press.

Tilly, C. (1998). *Durable inequality*. Berkeley, CA: University of California Press.

Tobias, S., Cole, C., Zibrin, M., & Bodlakova, V. (1982). Teacher–student ethnicity and recommendations for special education referrals. *Journal of Educational Psychology, 74*(1), 72.

Trainor, A. A., & Bal, A. (2014). Development and preliminary analysis of a rubric for culturally responsive research. *Journal of Special Education, 47*, 203–216.

Tyson, K. (Ed.). (2011). *Integration interrupted: Tracking, Black students, and acting White after Brown*. New York, NY: Oxford University Press.

Tyson, K., Darity Jr, W., & Castellino, D. R. (2005). It's not "a black thing": Understanding the burden of acting white and other dilemmas of high achievement. *American Sociological Review, 70*(4), 582–605.

U.S. Department of Education. (2009). Children with disabilities receiving special education under Part B of the Individuals with Disabilities Education Act (Office of Special Education Programs, Data Analysis Systems, OMB No. 1820-0043). Washington, DC: Author.

U.S. Government Accountability Office (GAO). (2013). Individuals with Disabilities Education Act: Standards needed to improve identification of racial and ethnic overrepresentation in special education. Retrieved from www.gao.gov/products/GAO-13-137

Utley, C. A., Kozleski, E., Smith, A., & Draper, I. L. (2002). Positive behavior support: A pro-active strategy for minimizing behavior problems in urban multicultural youth. *Journal of Positive Behavior Interventions, 4*, 196–207.

Valencia, R. R. (2010). *Dismantling contemporary deficit thinking: Educational thought and practice*. New York, NY: Routledge.

Valencia, R. R. (Ed.). (2012). *The evolution of deficit thinking: Educational thought and practice*. New York, NY: Routledge.

Valencia, R. R., & Solórzano, D. G. (1997). Contemporary deficit thinking. In R. Valencia (Ed.), *The evolution of deficit thinking: Educational thought and practice*, 160–210. Abingdon, United Kingdom: RoutledgeFalmer.

Van Houtte, M. (2011). So where's the teacher in school effects research? The impact of teachers' beliefs, culture, and behavior on equity and excellence in education. In K. Van den Braden, P. Van Avermaet, & M. Van Houtte (Eds.), *Equity and excellence in education: Towards maximal learning opportunities for all students* (pp. 75–95). New York, NY: Routledge.

Vavrus, F., & Cole, K. (2002). "I didn't do nothin'": The discursive construction of school suspension. *Urban Review, 34*(2), 87–111.

Waitoller, F. R., Artiles, A. J., & Cheney, D. A. (2010). The miner's canary: A review of overrepresentation research and explanations. *Journal of Special Education, 44*(1), 29–49.

Waitoller, F. R., & Thorius, K. A. K. (2016). Cross-pollinating culturally sustaining pedagogy and universal design for learning: Toward an inclusive pedagogy that accounts for dis/ability. *Harvard Educational Review, 86*(3), 366–389.

Wakelin, M. M. (2008). Challenging disparities in special education: Moving parents from disempowered team members to ardent advocates. *Northwestern Journal of Law and Social Policy*, 3, 263.

Walker, H. M., Horner, R. H., Sugai, G., Bullis, M., Sprague, J. R., Bricker, D., & Kaufman, M. J. (1996). Integrated approaches to preventing antisocial behavior patterns among school-age children and youth. *Journal of Emotional and Behavioral Disorders*, 4(4), 194–209.

Warren, J. R., Sheridan, J. T., & Hauser, R. M. (2002). Occupational stratification across the life course: Evidence from the Wisconsin Longitudinal Study. *American Sociological Review*, 67, 432–455.

Weick, K. E. (1976). Educational organizations as loosely coupled systems. *Administrative Science Quarterly*, 1–19.

Wells, A. S. (2009). *Both sides now: The story of school desegregation's graduates*. Berkeley, CA: University of California Press.

Wells, A. S., Ready, D., Duran, J., Grzesikowski, C., Hill, K., Roda, A., . . . & White, T. (2012). Still separate, still unequal, but not always so "suburban." In W. F. Tate (Ed.), *Research on schools, neighborhoods, and communities: Toward civic responsibility* (pp. 125–149). Blue Ridge Summit, PA: Rowman & Littlefield.

Wells, T., Sandefur, G. D., & Hogan, D. P. (2003). What happens after the high school years among young persons with disabilities? *Social Forces*, 82(2), 803–832.

Welner, K. G. (2001). *Legal rights, local wrongs: When community control collides with educational equity*. Albany, NY: SUNY Press.

Welner, K. G., & Carter, P. L. (2013). Achievement gaps arise from opportunity gaps. In P. L. Carter & K. G. Welner (Eds.), *Closing the opportunity gap: What America must do to give every child an even chance* (pp. 1–10). New York, NY: Oxford University Press.

Winzer, M. A. (1993). *The history of special education: From isolation to integration*. Washington, DC: Gallaudet University Press.

Wrightslaw. (n.d.) Retrieved from www.wrightslaw.com/law/reports/IDEA_ Compliance_1.htm

Yell, M. L., Rogers, D., & Rogers, E. L. (1998). The legal history of special education: What a long, strange trip it's been! *Remedial and Special Education*, 19(4), 219–228.

Yell, M. L., Shriner, J. G., & Katsiyannis, A. (2006). Individuals with Disabilities Education Improvement Act of 2004 and IDEA regulations of 2006: Implications for educators, administrators, and teacher trainers. *Focus on Exceptional Children*, 39(1), 1.

Zirkel, P. A. (2005). Does *Brown v. Board of Education* play a prominent role in special education law? *Journal of Law and Education*, 34, 255.

Index

About the Author

Catherine Kramarczuk Voulgarides is an assistant professor of special education at Touro College in New York City, New York. She also works as an educational consultant, having worked in the field of education in New York City for more than a decade in multiple capacities. She has been a teacher, researcher, equity associate, senior research associate, and is now a professor. Her professional and academic work is focused on not only identifying inequities in practice, but also finding ways to address them. Her work is dedicated to connecting the insights of social theory to the realities of schools and districts.